Origami Ornaments

Origami Ornaments

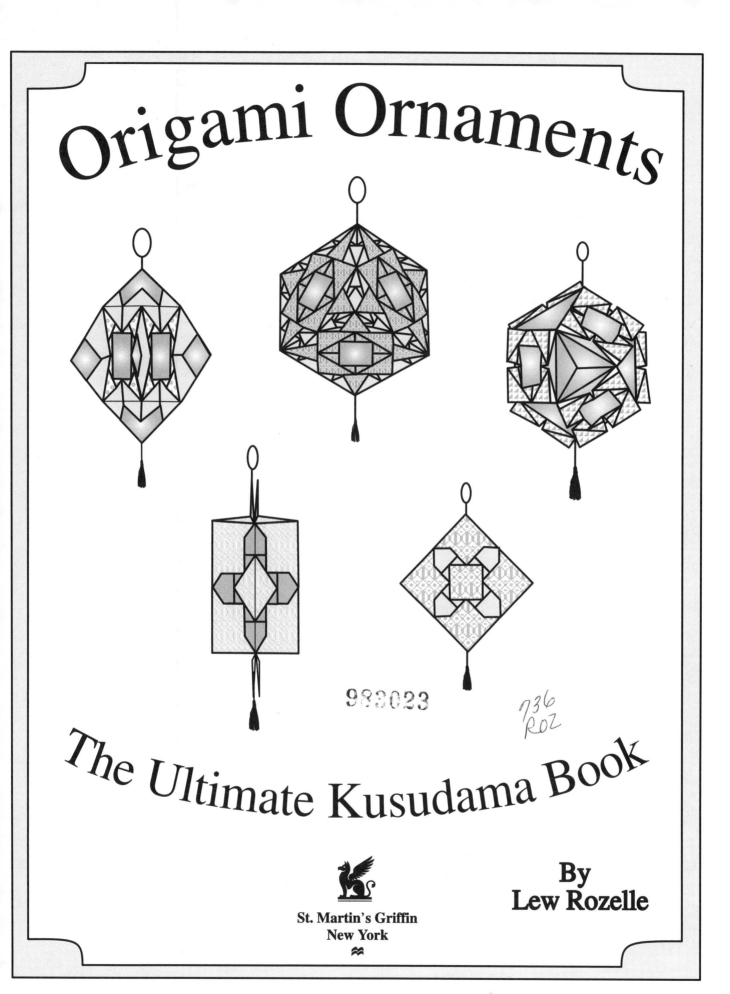

The Ultimate Kusudama Book

St. Martin's Griffin
New York

By
Lew Rozelle

www.stmartins.com

Production Editor: David Stanford Burr
Copy Editor: Sam Randlett
Design by Lew Rozelle

Library of Congress Cataloging-in-Publication Data

Rozelle, Lew.
  Origami ornaments : the ultimate kusudama book / by Lew Rozelle.— 1st ed.
    p. cm.
  ISBN 0-312-26369-4
  1. Origami.   2. Christmas tree ornaments. I. Title.

TT870 .R683 2000   00-040262

736'.982—dc21

First Edition: October 2000

10 9 8 7 6 5 4 3 2 1

Contents

Procedures

Simple Ornaments

Procedures

Complex Ornaments

Designing Ornaments

Units

Introduction

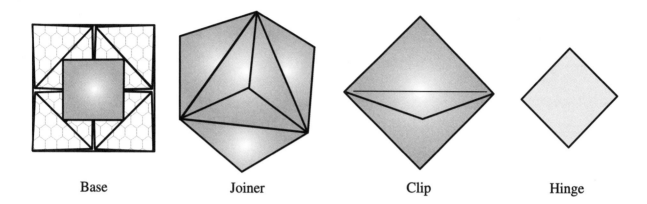

| Base | Joiner | Clip | Hinge |

At Christmas time almost half a century ago I tried to fold ornaments from gift wrap, but the paper was too thin and brittle to be practical. Over the years, however, I devised a set of units for making Christmas ornaments; gradually this developed into a logical system of modular origami using only four basic units. Each unit has many simple variations, and these can be combined into a very large number of ball-constructions.

Kusudama (Ball Origami Ornaments) are traditional in Japan, but almost all of them require glue. The ornaments here continue the Japanese tradition, but they are joined and locked solely by folding. The string loops that suspend the balls and the decorative tassels that give them an Asian feeling are also firmly attached without glue.

The models are arranged in order of complexity. The first ones are folded flat and then expanded; more complex balls later in the book must be assembled in three dimensions.

Small ornaments may hang on a Christmas tree, while larger ones can be filled with aromatic potpourri. When the Kusudama have rested for a time they open up; they do not come apart, but the modules open gently like flowers.

I hope you enjoy folding these paper ornaments as much as I have.

Lew Rozelle

Procedures

International symbols for folding paper

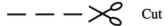

– – – – – – –   Valley Fold

· – · – · – · – · –   Mountain Fold

– – – ✂   Cut

Fold in Front

Fold Behind

Turn Model Over

Fold and Unfold

Apply Force

▶   Sink or Push In

●   Watch this Spot

X   Watch this Spot

○   Hold Here

Symbols

The symbols used in origami are shown at the left. They are the international language of the origami world.

A series of dashes represents a valley fold. Make a concave crease where this line appears.

A series of dots and dashes represents a mountain fold. Make a convex crease wherever this line appears.

A series of dashes with a pair of scissors indicates a cut.

Arrows will show the directions in which you make the fold: left, right, up, down, in front, behind and into. These directions have to do with the page itself. "Fold upward" means "fold toward the top of the page." "Near" is closest to you. "Far" or "behind" is away from you. There are also symbols for turning the model over and for tucking or opening a portion of the model.

Following Directions

There are three important directions given for each step in folding a model.

First, read the written instructions. "Valley-fold" tells you to make a valley fold. "Repeat steps 3–5" gives you instructions which would be difficult to convey in a drawing.

Second, look at the accompanying drawing. The drawing will show you how the model should look as each step in the folding takes place. The arrows will also help you see where to make a fold.

Third, always look ahead to the next drawing. Look to see how the model should look after a fold is made. This will also show you when you have made a mistake. You should go on folding only after you have completed the step successfully.

Procedures

There are several combinations of folds, which when combined produce a desired effect. "Reverse-fold" is a procedure which has several folding steps. These will be explained in the next few pages, before you begin folding. Remember to make each fold as precise as you can.

Paper

The ornaments in this book were designed to be made from Christmas wrapping paper. They can be made from origami paper, but you will enjoy making paper squares from the wide assortment of gift wraps. Here is how to fold and cut the gift wrap into squares that can then be folded into ornaments.

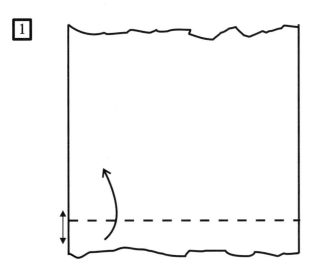

Begin with a section of gift wrap or the end on a roll. Valley-fold the edge of the paper up and align one side of the straight edges perfectly.

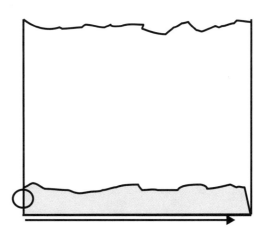

Hold the aligned edges together and form a crease from left to right. Keep the folded edge from wrinkling as you make the crease.

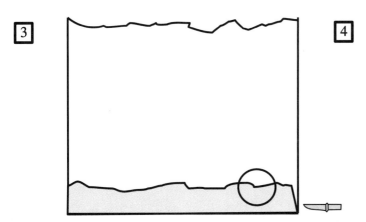

Hold down the two layers and carefully cut away the near layer using a plastic picnic knife or letter opener. Make the cut as straight as possible along the crease formed in step 2.

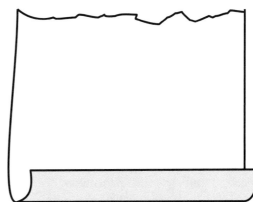

You now have straight edges on the bottom and sides of the paper. Repeat steps 1 and 2 with the new bottom edge until you have the size needed to make a row of squares.

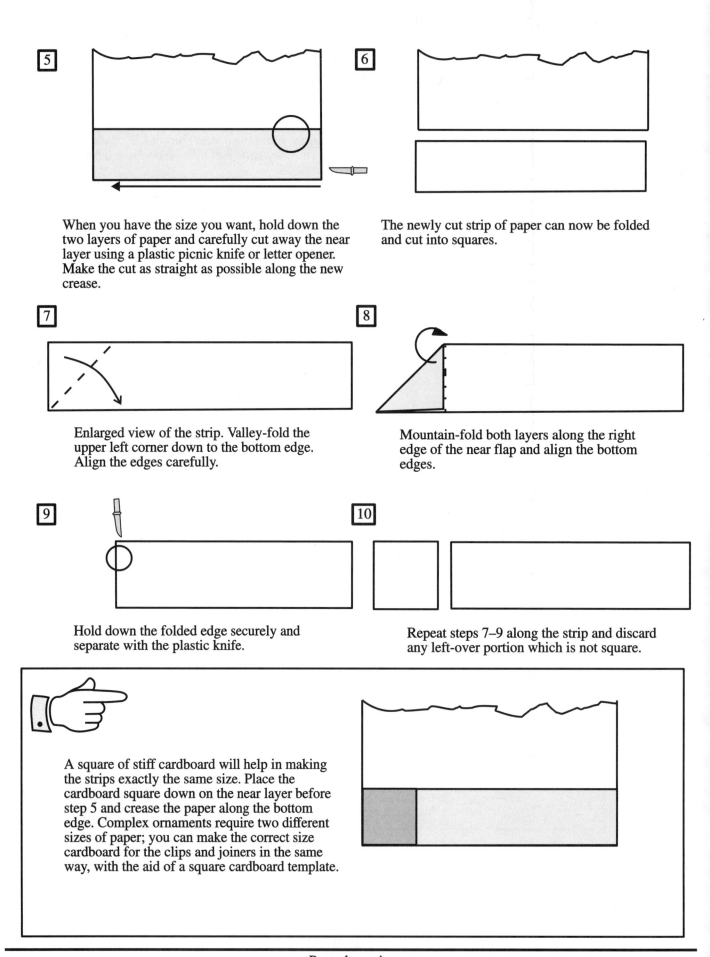

5 When you have the size you want, hold down the two layers of paper and carefully cut away the near layer using a plastic picnic knife or letter opener. Make the cut as straight as possible along the new crease.

6 The newly cut strip of paper can now be folded and cut into squares.

7 Enlarged view of the strip. Valley-fold the upper left corner down to the bottom edge. Align the edges carefully.

8 Mountain-fold both layers along the right edge of the near flap and align the bottom edges.

9 Hold down the folded edge securely and separate with the plastic knife.

10 Repeat steps 7–9 along the strip and discard any left-over portion which is not square.

A square of stiff cardboard will help in making the strips exactly the same size. Place the cardboard square down on the near layer before step 5 and crease the paper along the bottom edge. Complex ornaments require two different sizes of paper; you can make the correct size cardboard for the clips and joiners in the same way, with the aid of a square cardboard template.

Simple Ornaments
Procedures

The different folds that you will use in this section are explained in the next few pages.

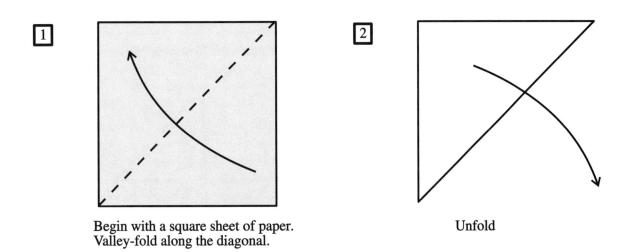

1 Begin with a square sheet of paper. Valley-fold along the diagonal.

2 Unfold

Each of the drawings in this book represents a folding procedure. Follow each step carefully until you have completed a sequence. The drawing at the left shows a simple valley fold. Notice that the square is shaded; this indicates that the colored side of the paper is showing. The dashed line indicates where the fold should be made; the crease will form a valley. Try to be as precise as you can so that the edges of the paper align.

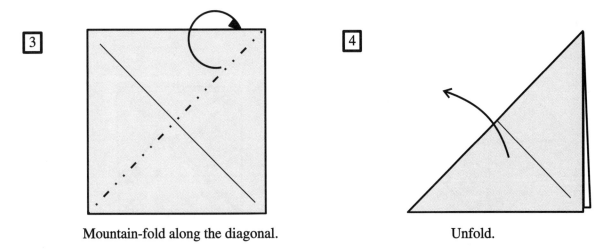

3 Mountain-fold along the diagonal.

4 Unfold.

The mountain fold is indicated by a different type of line and arrow. The paper is folded behind. The drawings sometimes show the folded result in perspective so that we can see where the paper has gone after the crease has been formed—the edges will in fact be exactly aligned.

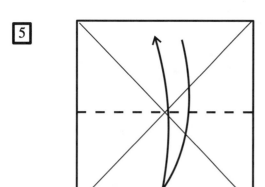

Valley-fold the paper in half and unfold.

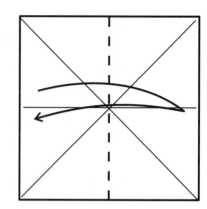

Valley-fold the paper in half and unfold.

Step 5 shows an arrow which indicates that the paper is folded and then unfolded. Step 6 shows the same procedure but the paper is folded in a different direction.

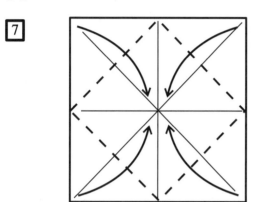

Valley-fold all of the corners to the center.

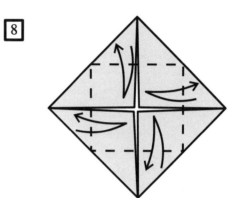

Valley-fold the corners to the center and unfold.

Step 7 shows that all four corners are folded inward to the center. The completed folds are shown in step 8. When all four corners have been folded to the center, a blintz fold has been formed. Step 8 shows that the four corners are again folded to the center and unfolded.

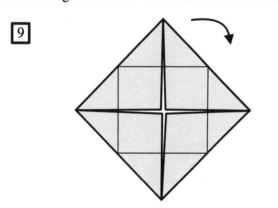

Rotate the unit so that it looks like step 10.

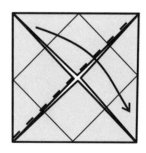

Valley-fold in half along the diagonal crease.

Step 9 shows the completed folds. Step 10 begins the next sequence of folds by indicating a fold along the diagonal crease.

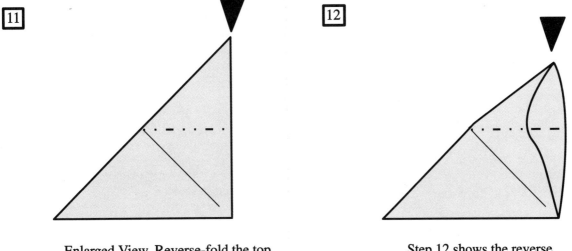

11

Enlarged View. Reverse-fold the top
corner into the paper.

12

Step 12 shows the reverse
fold in progress.

Step 11 shows an enlarged view; this makes it easier to see where to make the folds. The black triangle in step 11 indicates a reverse fold. You are going to reverse the direction of part of the existing mountain fold and move the corner of the paper inside, between the near and far layers. Step 12 shows this procedure in progress.

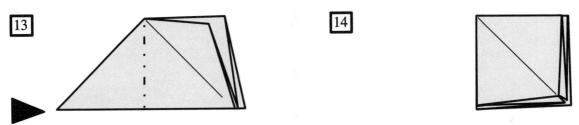

13

Reverse-fold the left corner into the paper.

14

The completed unit forms what is
know as a Preliminary Fold.

Making the reverse fold shown in steps 11 and 12 has brought the top point down inside. Step 13 shows the completed fold and shows the notation for repeating this process on the left corner.

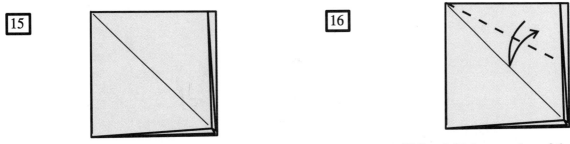

15

Enlarged view of step 14.

16

Valley-fold the top edge of the near flap
down to the crease line and unfold.

Step 15 shows the result of the folds completed so far. The configuration that has been created is called a Preliminary Fold. It is used to form the Joiners and Clips in this book. Steps 15–16 show an enlarged view and begin another type of procedure called a squash fold.

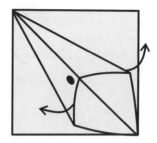

Lift the near flap toward yourself and squash-fold
the top near corner along the crease
formed in step 16. Watch the black dot.

Step 18 shows the squash fold in progress.
Allow the flap to open out along the crease
formed in step 16.

Step 17 shows the beginning of a squash fold. The flap is going to be opened symmetrically and then pressed
flat. Step 18 shows this procedure in progress.

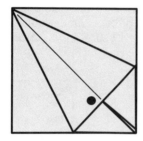

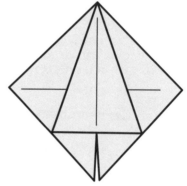

The completed squash fold.
Repeat steps 16–18 behind.

This modified Preliminary Fold
can be folded into a Joiner or a Clip.

The completed squash fold has flattened the near flap of step 17 onto the model. By repeating this procedure on the
back of the paper (behind) you have created a unit which will find use as a Clip for making an ornament.

You will find hints throughout this book. They will appear when a suggestion may help
you through a difficult procedure or when an explanation will help figure out a problem
during assembly.

The Preliminary Fold shown in step 14 is
used for making different variations of
Clips and Joiners.

Base

Before you begin an ornament it is necessary to learn four units. The first is the foundation for all of the ornaments in this book. Steps 5 and 6 allow the parts of the ornament to be locked together without the use of glue. Although there seem to be many steps in making this simple base, every step will make the final assembly of the ornament easier and more accurate.

 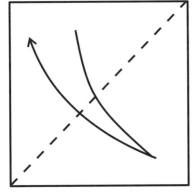

Begin with a square sheet of paper. Valley-fold along the diagonal and unfold.

 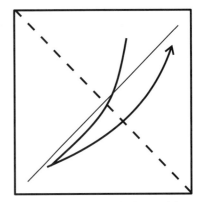

Valley-fold in half along the other diagonal and unfold.

 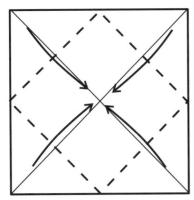

Blintz-fold the paper by valley-folding all the corners to the center.

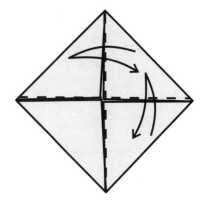

Valley-fold along the diagonals and unfold.

 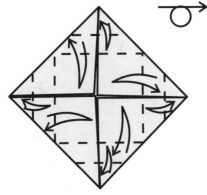

Fold all corners to the center and unfold; then valley-fold all the corners to the creases and unfold. **Turn the model over.**

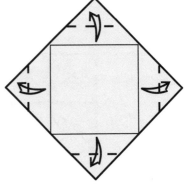

Valley-fold all the corners to the first creases formed in step 5 and crease hard. **Unfold the paper completely.**

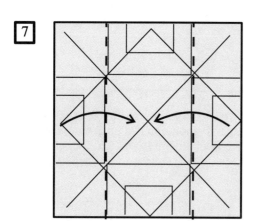

With the colored side up, valley-fold the sides to the center.

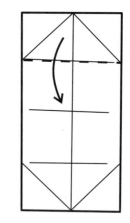

Valley-fold the top edge to the center.

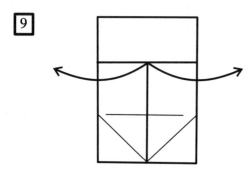

Grasp the two inner corners and gently pull them outward as far as they will go. Look ahead to step 10. Flatten the unit.

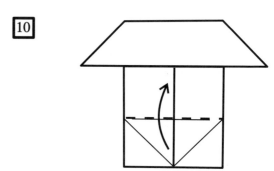

Repeat steps 8 and 9 on the bottom half.

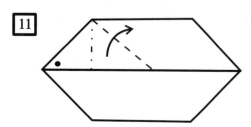

Lift the near top left corner of the base. Open and squash-fold it down flat along the existing creases. Watch the black dot.

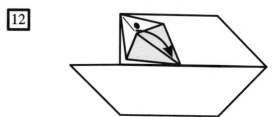

Step 12 shows this folding in progress. Flatten the opened flap. Repeat step 11 on the three remaining corners.

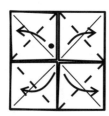

Valley-fold the central corners of the near flaps to the corners of the unit.

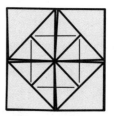

The completed Base has four large pockets on each side. These will be used to connect the different parts of the ornaments and hold them together.

Clip

This unit allows two bases to be joined. Steps 5 and 6 allow the parts of the ornament to be locked together without the use of glue. The first steps are the same as those for the Base and will make the final assembly of the ornament easier and more accurate.

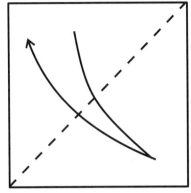

1

Begin with a square sheet of paper.
Valley-fold along the diagonal and unfold.

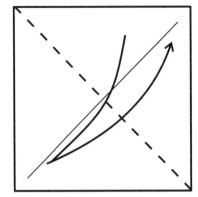

2

Valley-fold in half along the
other diagonal and unfold.

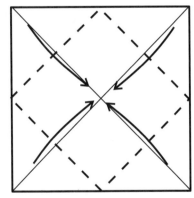

3

Blintz-fold the paper by valley-folding
all the corners to the center.

4

Blintz-fold and unfold.

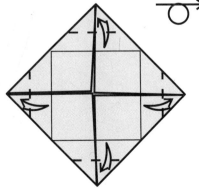

5

Valley-fold and unfold all the corners to
the creases formed in step 4 and crease
hard. **Turn the model over.**

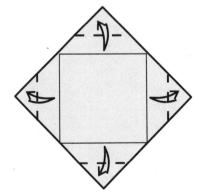

6

Valley-fold and unfold all the corners
to the creases formed in step 4 and
crease hard.

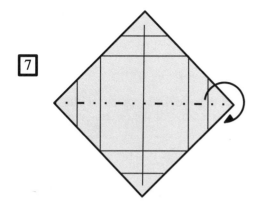

7

Mountain-fold the top to the bottom.

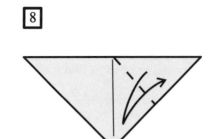

8

Valley-fold the right point down to the bottom corner and unfold.

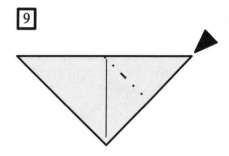

9

Reverse-fold the right corner into the paper.

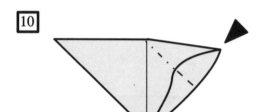

10

Step 10 shows the reverse fold in progress.

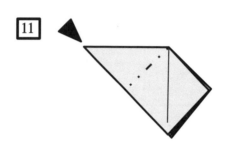

11

Repeat steps 8–10 on the remaining corner.

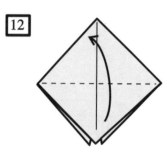

12

Enlarged view. Valley-fold the bottom point of the near flap up to the top.

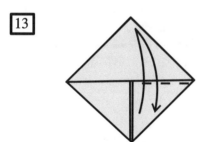

13

Valley-fold the point of the lower right inner flap up to the top point and unfold.

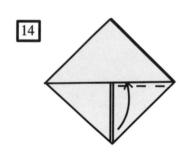

14

Valley-fold the lower right flap up into the Clip.

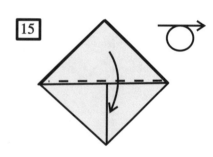

15

Swing the near top layer down. **Turn the model over from left to right.**

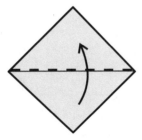

16

Repeat steps 12–15 to complete the Clip.

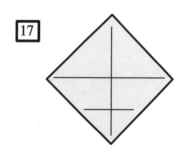

17

The bottom flaps, front and back, are now accessible for the locking together of two bases.

Joiner

This unit allows three Bases to be joined. Steps 5 and 6 allow the parts of the ornament to be locked without glue. Every step will make the final assembly of the ornament easier and more accurate.

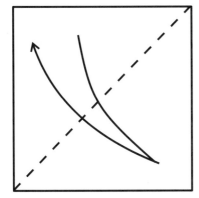

Begin with a square sheet of paper.
Valley-fold along the diagonal and unfold.

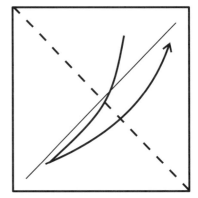

Valley-fold in half along the
other diagonal and unfold.

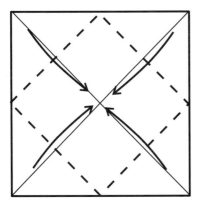

Blintz-fold the paper by valley-folding
all the corners to the center.

Blintz-fold and unfold.

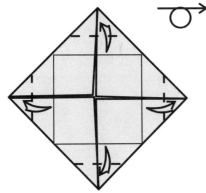

Valley-fold and unfold all the corners to
the creases formed in step 4 and crease
hard. **Turn the model over.**

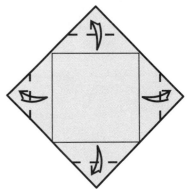

Valley-fold all the corners to the creases
formed in step 4 and crease hard. **Unfold
the paper completely.**

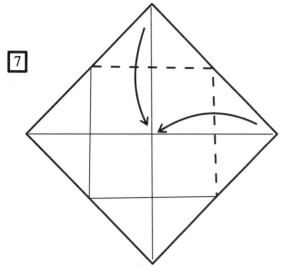

7 Place the paper colored side down. Valley-fold the top and right corners to the center.

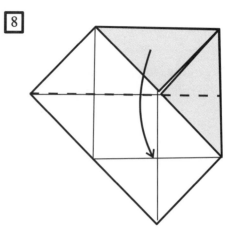

8 Valley-fold the the model downward in half.

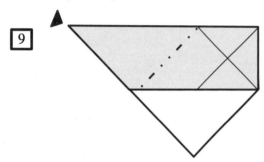

9 Reverse-fold the left flap downward.

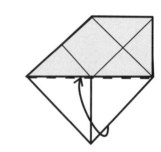

10 Valley-fold the two lower flaps upward as one, into the upper half of the unit.

 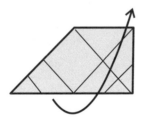

11 Open out the Joiner and reposition so the open end is down and the central peak is up.

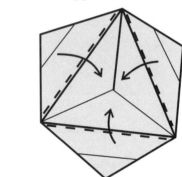

12 The Joiner is seen here in an enlarged view from the top. Valley-fold each of the side flaps to the central peak of the pyramid, and gently unfold them partway. These three side flaps allow three bases to be joined together.

 The Joiner shown above forms a small pyramid or raised triangular shape when assembled as a part of an ornament. Step 11 opens the Joiner. There are small triangular flaps on the three sides. These will connect the Joiner to a Base and will allow the ornament to be assembled without glue. (The Joiner can also be folded so that the center area is concave. The folding is slightly different and will be covered later in the book.)

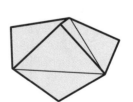

3-D View

Hinge

This model allows two Bases to be joined. Steps 5 and 6 allow the parts of the ornament to be locked together without glue. Every step will make the final assembly of the ornament easier and more accurate.

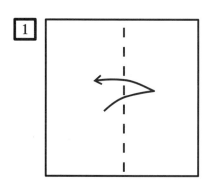

1 Valley-fold the right edge over to the left edge and unfold.

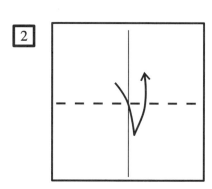

2 Valley-fold the top edge down to the bottom edge and unfold.

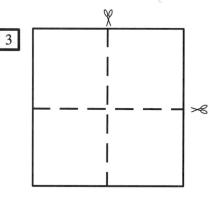

3 Cut the paper along the crease lines formed in steps 1–2.

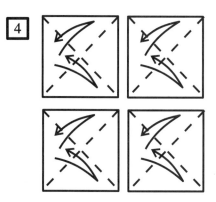

4 Valley-fold and unfold each square on the diagonals.

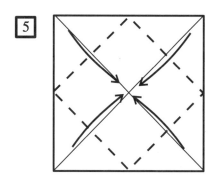

5 Enlarged view of a single square from step 4. Blintz-fold the paper by valley-folding all the corners to the center.

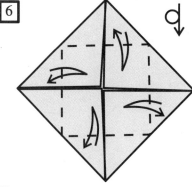

6 Blintz-fold and unfold. **Turn the model over.**

 Hinges are the simplest means of joining two Bases together. When you begin to make the ornaments, remember that Clips join two Bases together and add a third dimension to the ornament. When you need to join two Bases but do not want an added dimension, or when you wish to hide the joint, use a Hinge.

Lantern using a Clip.   Lantern using a Hinge.

Inserts

The use of contrasting colors and foils makes great looking ornaments. Inserts are simply small squares of paper added to Bases, Clips and Joiners to add variety to the ornaments.

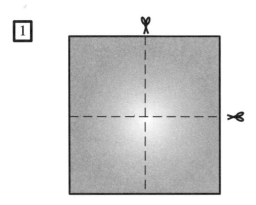

Begin with a square the same size as the Hinge. Divide the paper again in the same way as the Hinge.

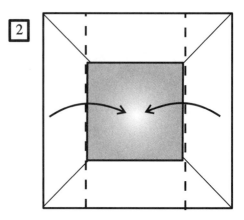

When the Base has been assembled into an ornament the Insert will be exposed.

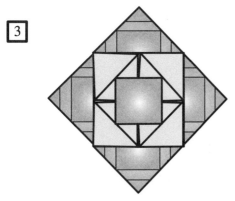

Fold a Base up to step 7. Place the small square from step 1 in the center of the Base and continue folding the Base with the Insert in place.

 Try to fold the Inserts from the same contrasting color paper as the Hinges, Clips, and Joiners.

Locking

All of the units lock together without glue, using the same method. If you have not done so already, make a Base, a Clip, a Joiner, and a Hinge. Label each of these units and keep the labeled set handy for reference. Try locking several modules together and unlocking them before you attempt to construct an ornament.

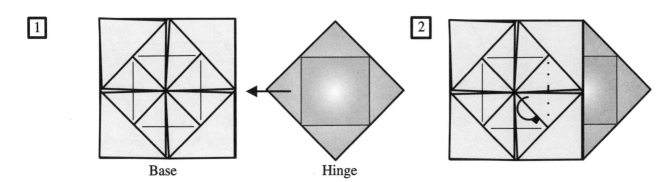

Base   Hinge

Slide the corner of a Hinge into one of the side pockets of a Base. Center the Hinge within the pocket.

Mountain-fold the inside right flap of the Base— the flap that contains the corner of the Hinge — along the existing creases. This will lock the two modules together. Flatten the fold and you are ready to add another module to the base.

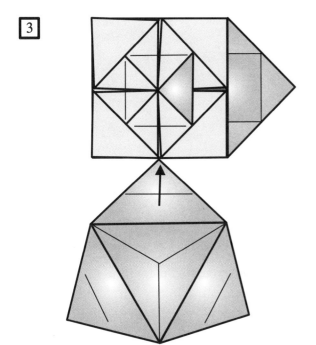

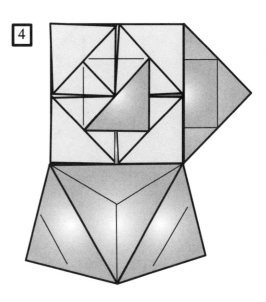

Repeat steps 1 and 2 to lock a Joiner to the Base. The central peak of the Joiner points toward us in steps 3 and 4.

Modules can be locked and unlocked to make adjustments in the Ornament.

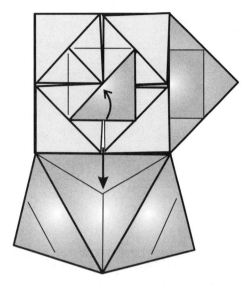

 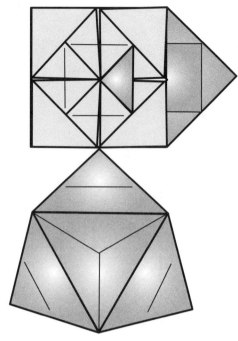

Now unlock the Joiner from the Base by unfolding the inner flaps.

Modules can be locked and unlocked to make adjustments in the ornament.

 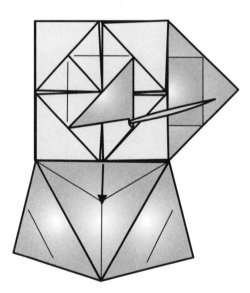

You may want to try using a toothpick or other small object to lift the inner flap in order to unlock the parts. A small pair of tweezers is helpful in locking and unlocking. From time to time you will find that the parts are not locked together exactly. By unlocking and adjusting the flaps, you can improve the appearance of the ornament.

String Loops and Tassels

You can fasten a string loop into a Base, Clip or Joiner in order to hang the ornament. A tassel can be added to the bottom of the ornament using the same proceedures.

1

Tie a loop at the end of a string to hang the ornament.

2

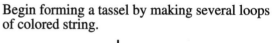

Begin forming a tassel by making several loops of colored string.

3

Tie the string in the center with a string long enough to hang from the ornament.

4

Tie all the loops together close to the hanging string. Cut the loops free at the bottom of the tassel.

5

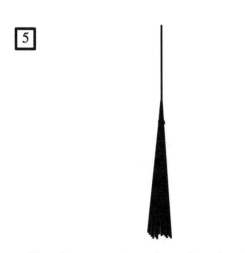

Tassels are easy to make and can be added to most of the ornaments.

6

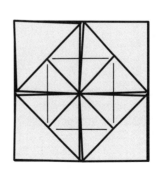

Adding the string to an ornament is fairly simple. Begin with a Base.

7

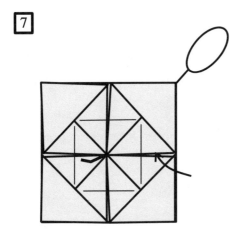

Insert the end of the looped string into the side flap of a Base. Be sure that the string is next to the fold and that a small portion extends out of the flap. You may leave as much of the looped end hanging out as you wish.

8

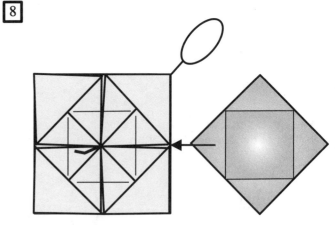

Insert a Hinge into the side of the Base with the string in position, and lock the two modules together.

9

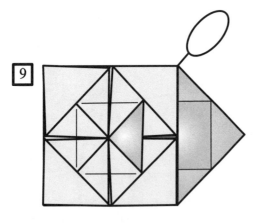

When the two parts are locked together the string is trapped inside the flaps and can be used to hang the ornament. This same process is used when attaching a Tassel to the ornament.

10

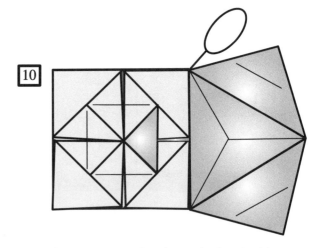

The same procedure is used when locking a Joiner onto a Base.

You may add as many tassels to an ornament as you wish. There are Lantern ornaments where you can add tassels to the sides and bottom.

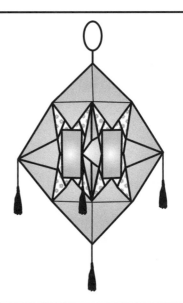

Simple Ornaments

Two-Dimensional Icon

This first ornament requires seven squares of paper the same size. Fold two Bases. Then, using foil or paper of a contrasting color, fold four Clips and divide the fifth into Inserts for the Bases. Fold the Bases with the Inserts in place.

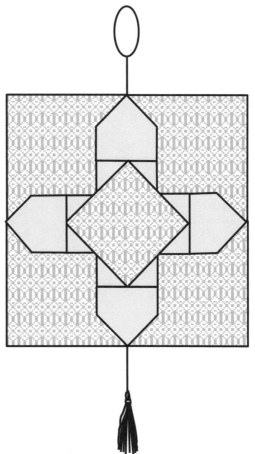

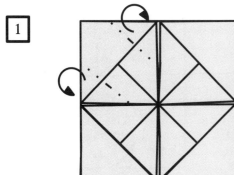

Begin with a Base. Mountain-fold the outer corners of the top near left flap inward as far as they will go. Repeat these folds on the three remaining flaps.

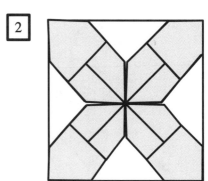

The finished folds make a pattern on the Base but will still allow a Clip to be folded onto the Base. You will need to repeat step 1 with the second Base.

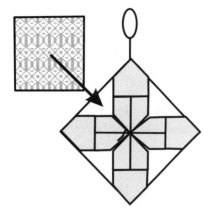

Insert a looped string under the top left flap of the Base so that the very end sticks out from the center; then insert the near flap of a Clip into the side of the Base and lock securely.

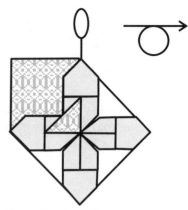

Turn the model over.

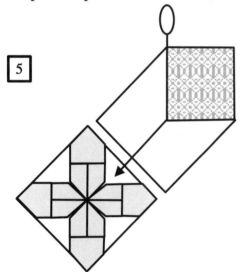

Insert the Clip (now on the near side of the step 4 construction) into the side of a second Base and lock it. The Base from step 4 will go behind the second Base.

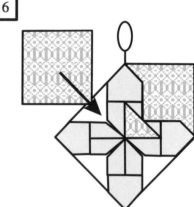

Insert and lock a second Clip, being careful to keep the flap on the back of the Clip in the far pocket of the Base. Lock in place.

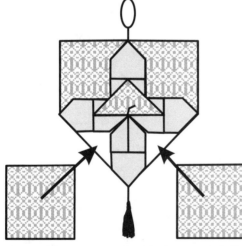

Insert a string with a tassel under the bottom left flap of the Base so the very end sticks out from the center. The Clips lock into place both in the back and in the front. Insert the third Clip into the Base front and back and lock in place. Insert the fourth Clip into the Base front and back and lock in place.

The Icon should look exactly the same on both sides.

Three-Dimensional Icon

This ornament requires seven squares of paper the same size. Fold two Bases as for the Two-Dimensional Icon (page 23, step1). Then, using foil or paper of a contrasting color, fold four Hanging Joiners (instructions below) and divide the fifth into Inserts for the Bases. Fold the Bases with the Inserts in place.

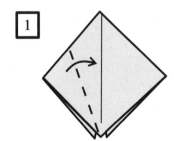

Begin a Hanging Joiner with step 11 of the Clip (pages 11–12). Valley-fold the lower left edge over to the centerline.

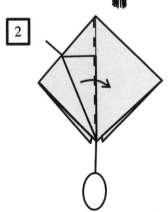

Insert a looped string under the nearest flap and place it directly into the crease at the left. Valley-fold the entire near left flap to the right over the centerline along with the string.

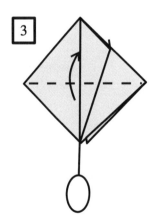

Continue forming the Joiner by valley-folding the bottom point of the near flap up to the top. Make a second Joiner with a string and tassel. Repeat steps 1–3 on the two remaining Joiners but without strings.

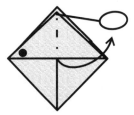

Pull the center of the near flap up and to the right, opening up the far left flap. Watch the black dot.

The open side of the module must be facing the center of the Base: see step 7.

 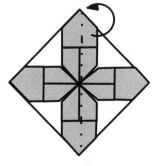

Mountain-fold and unfold both Bases as shown and crease hard. Unfold.

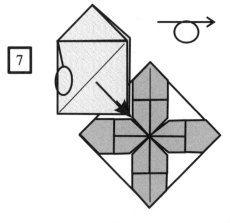

Insert a flap of the Joiner into the side of a Base and lock it into place. Make sure that the open side of the Joiner is facing the center of the Base; be sure the crease formed in the Base in step 6 runs up and down. **Turn the model over.**

 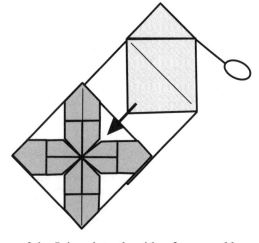

Fasten the flaps of the Joiner into the side of a second base and lock it using the method explained in step 7. The Base from step 7 goes behind the second Base.

 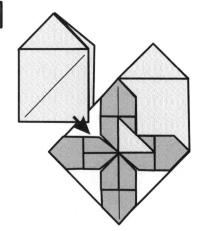

Repeat steps 7 and 8 with a second Joiner, being careful to keep the flap on the back of the Joiner in the pocket of the Base on the back. This Joiner does not need a string.

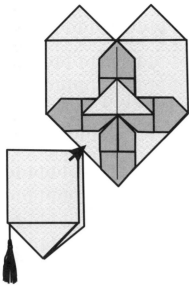
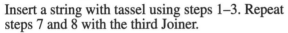

Insert a string with tassel using steps 1–3. Repeat steps 7 and 8 with the third Joiner.

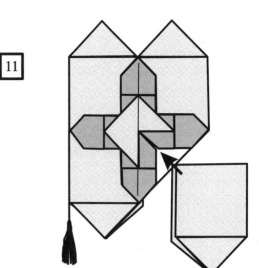

Repeat steps 7 and 8 with the fourth Joiner.

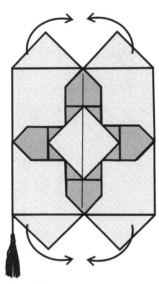

Gently squeeze the sides of the Icon to open out the two Bases along the heavy creases while bringing the modified flaps top and bottom toward the horizontal.

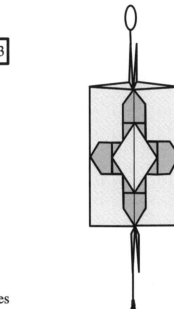

 Flaps on the Base can be opened to insert the flap of a Clip, or Joiner. This helps when a model has been folded without the flap already in place. Insert the Clip or Joiner and then return the Base flaps to their former positions.

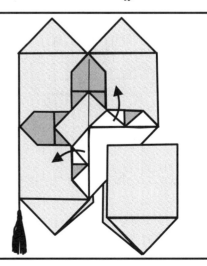

Three-Dimensional Icon 27

Cushion

This ornament requires ten squares of paper the same size. Fold three Bases as for the Two-Dimensional Icon (page 23, step1). Then, using foil or paper of a contrasting color, fold six Clips and divide the seventh into Inserts for the Bases. Fold the Bases with the Inserts in place.

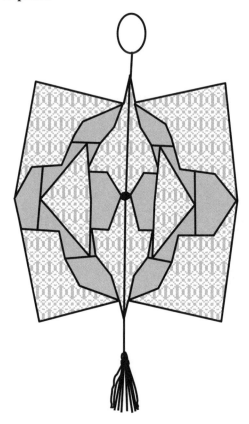

Mountain-fold the Base in half from right to left.

 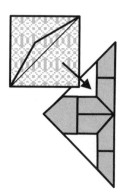

Insert a flap of a Clip into the side of a Base and lock. Repeat behind using a second Clip.

Insert and lock two more Clips onto the Base.

 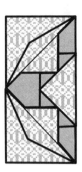

You should now have a single Base with four Clips attached.

Fasten the sides of a second Base onto the Clips of the assembly from step 4. The near flap of the Clip locks into the front pocket and the far flap locks into the pocket behind.

The assembly with two Bases and four attached Clips.

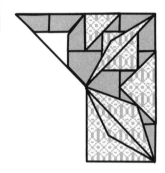 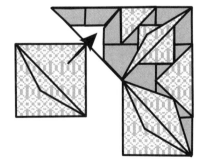 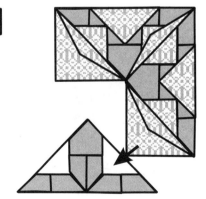

Attach two more Clips to the second Base; one locks into the near pocket and the second locks into the pocket behind.

Repeat step 5 with the third and last Base.

The assembly is almost complete. Pick up the model and cup it in your hand. Bring the second and third Bases together, "inflating" the model into three dimensions.

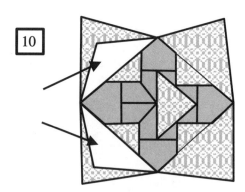

The two arrows show where the last two flaps are located. Insert them into the Base while you hold the sides of the model together.

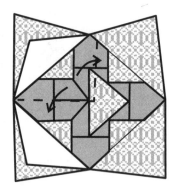

The action of step 10 is shown here in progress. Open the flaps of the Base on one side to allow the flap of the Clip to be inserted.

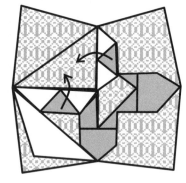

The action of step 10 continues. Place the Clip flap flush with the Base and fold the inner flaps of the Base back down over the Clip flap.

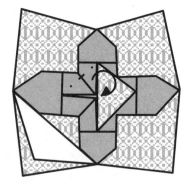

Lock the Clip and Base together. Repeat steps 11 through 13 on the remaining flap.

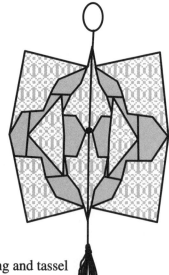

The looped string and tassel are optional.

Where's Up?

This model requires seven squares of paper the same size. Fold four Bases for the Two-Dimensional Icon (page 23, step 1). Then, using foil or paper of a contrasting color, fold eight Hinges and four Inserts for the Bases. Fold the Bases with the Inserts in place.

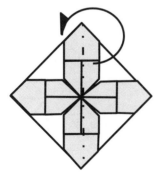

1 Mountain-fold the Base in half from right to left.

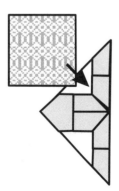

2 Insert a Hinge into the side of a Base and lock. Repeat on the back using a second Hinge.

Fasten two more Hinges onto the Base, one in front and one in back.

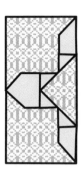

You now have a single Base with four Hinges attached.

Mountain-fold two more Bases from right to left, crease heavily, and unfold.

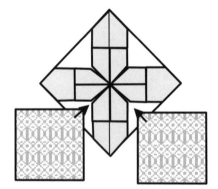

Be certain that the heavy crease runs up and down. Fasten two Hinges onto the lower two pockets of one Base and lock.

Turn the model over.

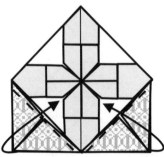

Place the remaining Base from step 5 onto the completed assembly of step 8. **Be sure the crease made in step 5 runs up and down.** Valley-fold the Hinges from the Base behind into this second Base and lock.

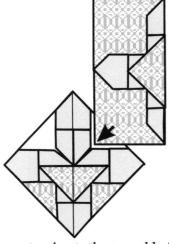

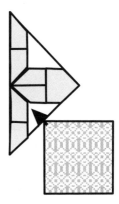

Lock the assembly from step 4 onto the assembly from step 8. The near Hinge locks onto the near Base, the Hinge behind locks onto the Base behind.

Fasten two more Hinges into the sides of the fourth Base, one in front and one behind.

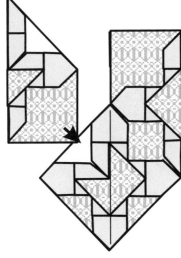

Lock the assembly from step 10 onto the assembly from step 9.

Hold the assembly in your hand and squeeze the two sides together, opening the ornament. Turn the top of the model toward yourself so that you can work from above.

Fold the two remaining Hinge flaps into the Base and lock securely, using the procedure shown at the end of the Cushion.

The looped string and tassel are optional.

Base Cube

Fold six Bases before making the Cube.

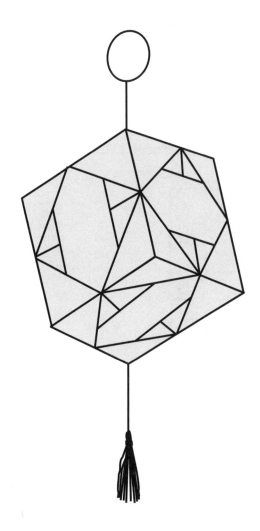

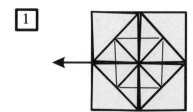

1. Begin with a Base. Open it slightly and pull the left internal flap all the way out to the left and rearrange it, flattening the flap into the position shown in step 2.

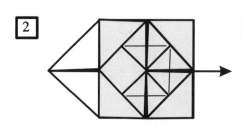

2. Treat the right internal flap in the same way.

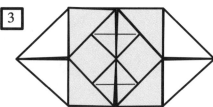

3. The Base now has two opposite external flaps and two opposite internal pockets. Repeat steps 1 and 2 with a total of six Bases.

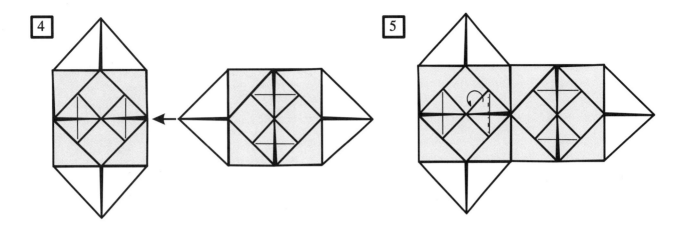

Begin assembling the Cube by inserting an external flap of the first Base into a pocket of second.

Mountain-fold the internal flap back inside the Base and lock in place.

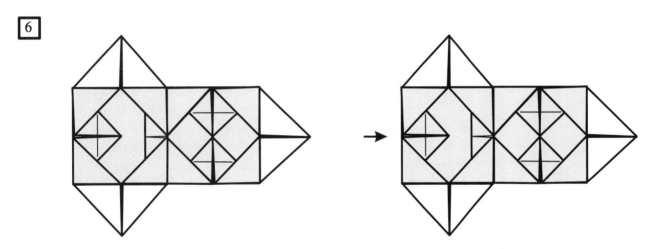

Repeat steps 4 and 5 on two more Bases. Join the two assemblies using the same method shown in steps 4 and 5.

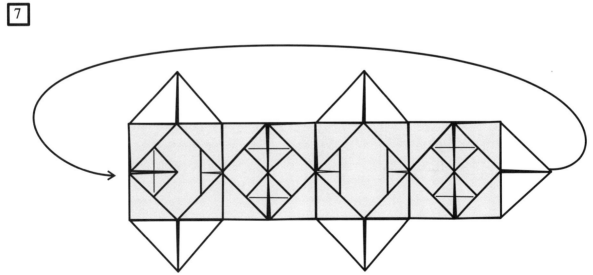

Swing the far right end of the assembly backward to the left; lock the right flap into the left Base using the procedure shown in steps 4 and 5. The result is an open box.

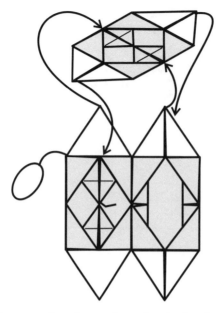

If you plan to hang the Cube from a string, insert the string before beginning this step. Add a top to the Cube by locking a fifth Base to the assembly. The same method of joining the Bases shown in steps 4 and 5 is used on these four flaps.

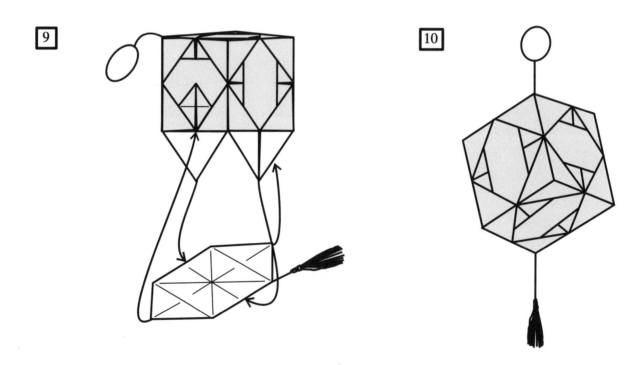

9

Add a bottom to the Cube by locking together the final Base to the assembly as in step 8. If you are going to add a tassel, add it now.

Four-Star Cube

This ornament requires eleven squares of paper the same size. Fold six Bases. Then, using foil or paper of a contrasting color, fold twelve Hinges from three squares. Cut two squares into eight inserts for the Bases. Two inserts will be left over after assembly. Fold the Bases with the Inserts in place. Two Hinges will be left over.

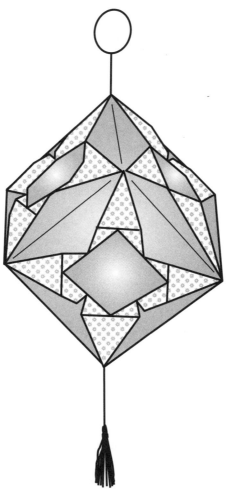

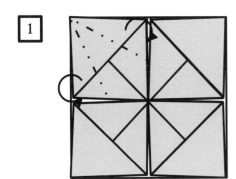

1 Begin with a Base (shown here in gray). Mountain-fold the outer edges of the top near left flap in as far as they will go.

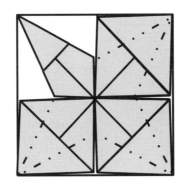

2 Repeat step 1 on the three remaining flaps.

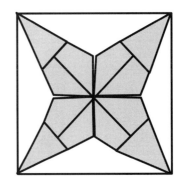

3 The finished folds will still allow a Hinge to be folded onto the module. Fold the remaining five Bases in the same way.

4

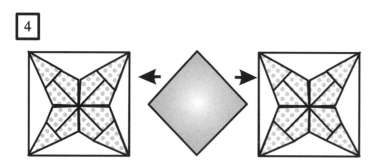

Insert a Hinge into the sides of two Bases and lock.

5

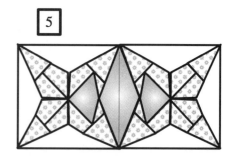

Repeat step 4 with another Hinge and two more Bases.

6

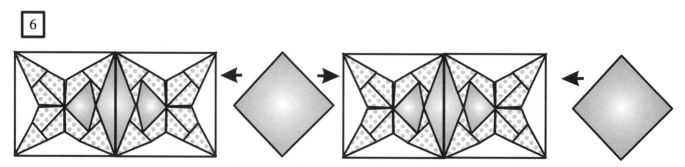

Fasten together the two existing assemblies with another Hinge. Insert a Hinge at the right and lock.

7

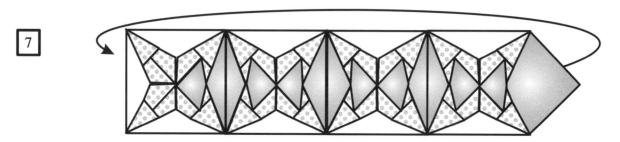

Swing the far right end of the assembly backward to the left; insert and lock the right Hinge into the left Base, completing an open box.

8

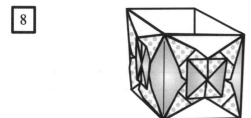

The open box needs to have a bottom and a lid to complete the Cube.

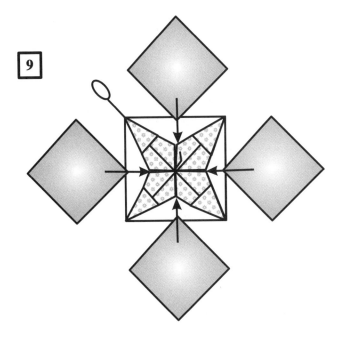

9

If you intend to hang the Cube, insert the string now. Insert and lock four Hinges into the fifth Base.

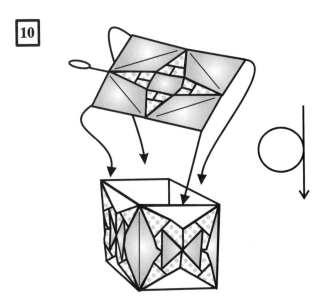

10

Insert and lock one of the Hinges from step 9 into the open top of the box formed in step 8. Continue to add a Hinge onto each side of the box. **Turn the box upside down.**

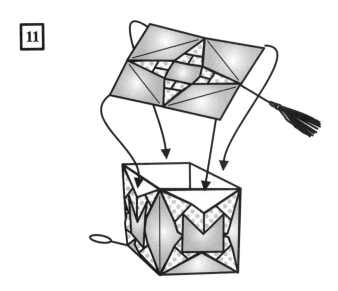

11

If you intend to have a tassel insert add it now. It should be at the opposite corner from the Loop. Repeat steps 9 and 10 to form the last side of the Cube.

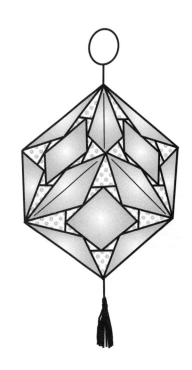

12

Cube

This ornament requires twenty squares of paper the same size. Fold six Bases. Then, using foil or paper of a contrasting color, fold twelve Clips. Cut six Inserts for the Bases. Fold the Bases with the Inserts in place. Two Inserts will be left over.

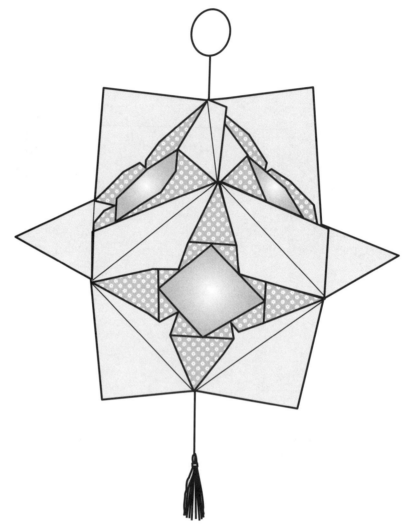

1

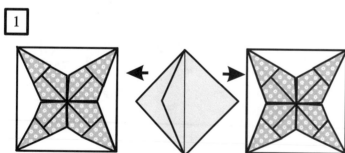

Prepare six Bases by mountain-folding their near flaps as in steps 1–3 of the Four-Sided Star Cube (page 37). Insert the right and left flaps of a Clip into the sides of two Bases and lock.

2

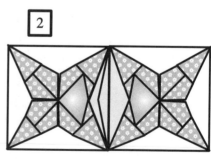

Repeat step 1 with a Clip and two more Bases.

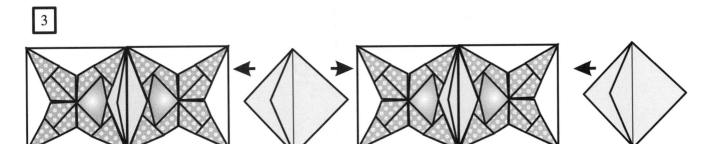

3

Fasten together the two existing assemblies with another Clip. Insert a fourth Clip at the right and lock.

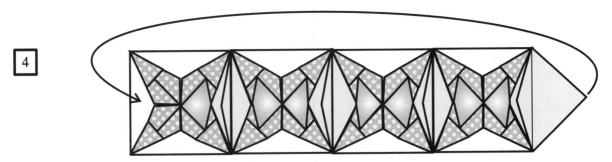

4

Swing the far right end of the assembly backward to the left; insert and lock the right Clip into the left Base, completing an open box.

5

The open box needs to have a bottom and lid to complete the Cube.

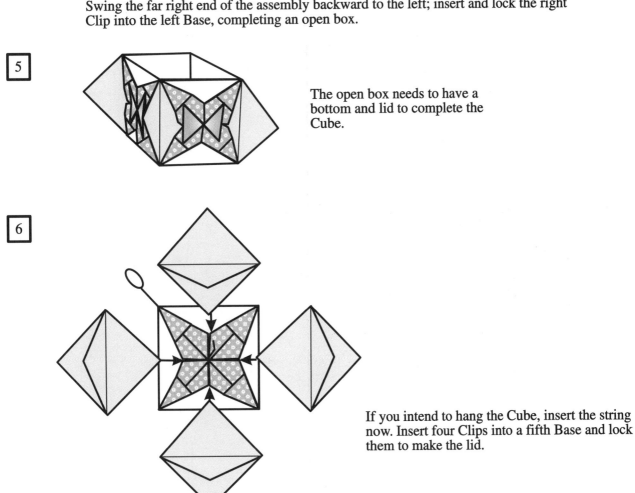

6

If you intend to hang the Cube, insert the string now. Insert four Clips into a fifth Base and lock them to make the lid.

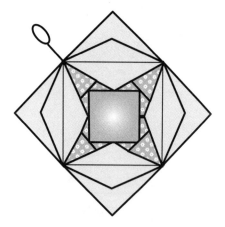

The completed lid can now be added to the sides of the Cube.

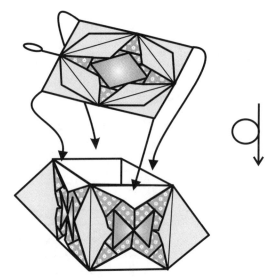

Insert one of the lid corners into a side of the box and lock. Continue to add a lid corner into each side of the box. **Turn the Cube upside down.**

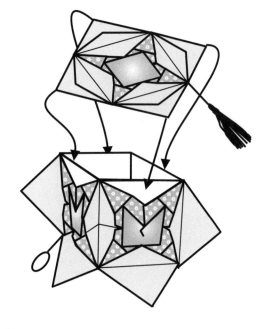

Repeat step 6–8 to form the last side of the Cube. If you intend to have a tassel, it should be at the opposite corner from the Loop.

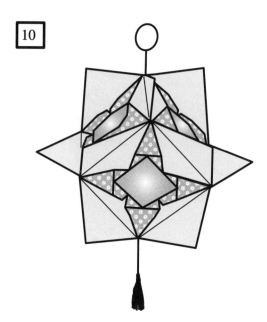

Magic Cube

This ornament requires fourteen squares of paper the same size. Fold six Bases as for the Two-Dimensional Icon (page 23, step1). Then, using foil or paper of a contrasting color, fold two Hanging Joiners (instructions below) and six Joiners.

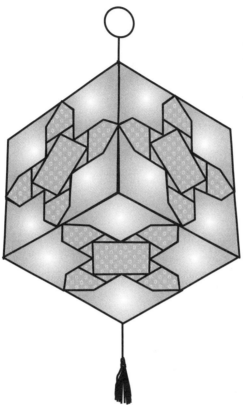

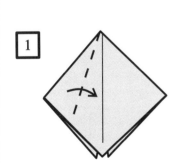

1. Form one Hanging Joiner (shown here in gray) by folding through step 12 of the Clip on page 12. Valley-fold the near left edge over to the centerline.

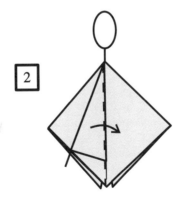

2. Insert a looped string under the nearest flap and place it directly into the crease at the left. Valley-fold the near left flap to the right over the centerline along with the string.

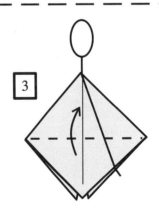

3. Valley-fold the bottom corner of the near flap up to the top, holding the string firmly in place. Repeat on the two remaining flaps. Open the Hanging Joiner when you are ready to lock it into the Cube.

4

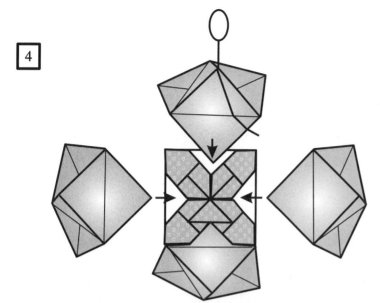

Insert into the top of a Base and lock into place the Hanging Joiner made in steps 1–3. Then add to the sides and bottom three normal Joiners, locking them in place.

5

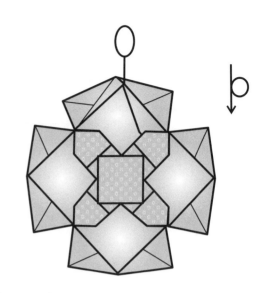

Turn the completed assembly over onto a flat surface with the Base on the bottom.

6

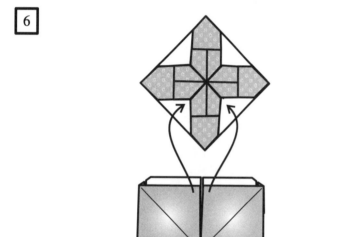

Add a Base to one side of the assembly.

7

Add a Base to each of the three remaining sides to form an open box.

8

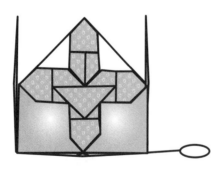

Keep the completed assembly on a flat surface with the Base on the bottom.

9

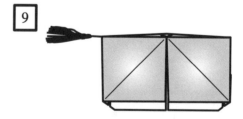

Complete another assembly by repeating steps 4 and 5. This assembly will form the last side of the Cube. You may wish to include a tassel on one of the Joiners opposite to the loop, using a Hanging Joiner as shown in steps 1–3.

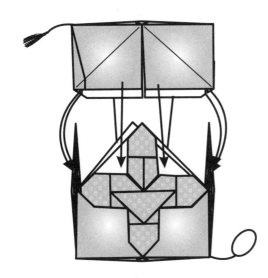

10

Add the completed assembly from step 9 by inserting and locking each flap securely.

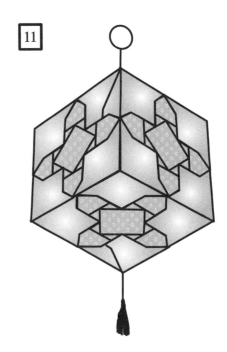

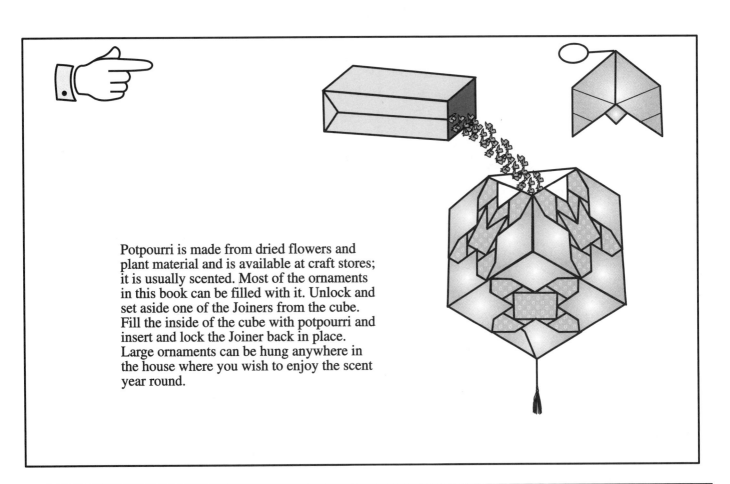

Potpourri is made from dried flowers and plant material and is available at craft stores; it is usually scented. Most of the ornaments in this book can be filled with it. Unlock and set aside one of the Joiners from the cube. Fill the inside of the cube with potpourri and insert and lock the Joiner back in place. Large ornaments can be hung anywhere in the house where you wish to enjoy the scent year round.

Ball Ornament

This ornament requires sixteen squares of paper the same size. Fold six Bases. Then, using foil or paper of a contrasting color, fold eight Concave Joiners (instructions below) and cut six Inserts for the Bases. Fold the Bases with the Inserts in place.

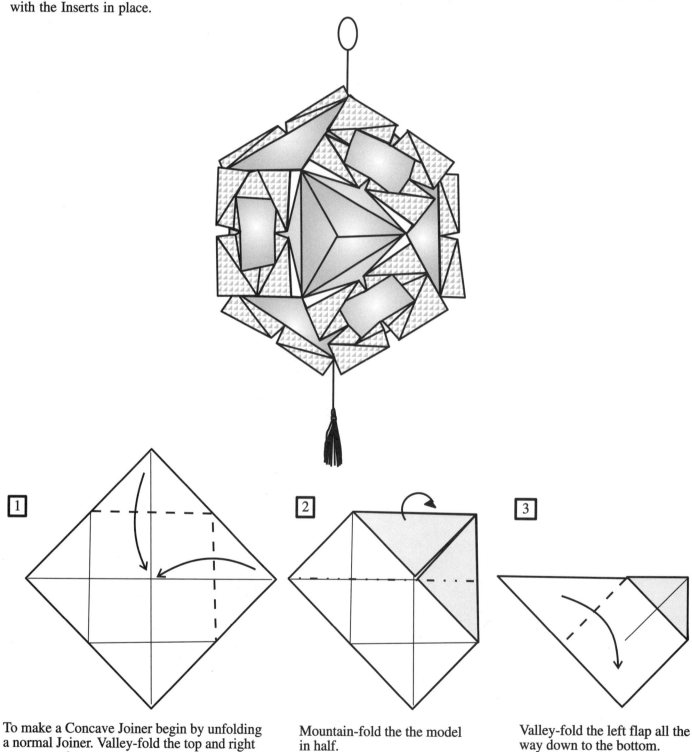

1

To make a Concave Joiner begin by unfolding a normal Joiner. Valley-fold the top and right corners to the center.

2

Mountain-fold the the model in half.

3

Valley-fold the left flap all the way down to the bottom.

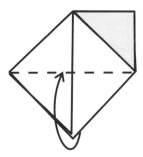

Valley-fold the two lower flaps up as one.

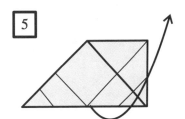

Open out the Joiner. In step 6 we are looking into a concave triangular bowl.

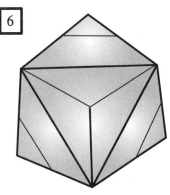

The Concave Joiner has three side flaps to allow three Bases to be joined together. Repeat steps 1–5 to form the seven remaining concave Joiners.

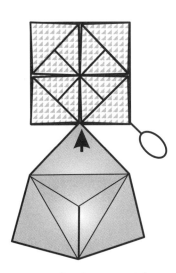

7

If you are going to use a string loop to hang the ornament, insert the string now. Begin assembling the Ball Ornament by sliding a corner of a Concave Joiner into the side of a Base.

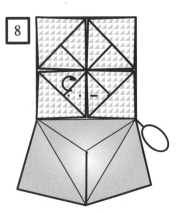

With the corner of the Joiner in the bottom pocket of the Base, mountain-fold the inside flap downward, locking the two units securely together.

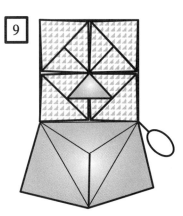

If you have made an Insert for the Base, the Insert color will begin to appear.

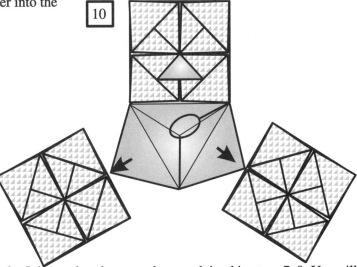

Join two more Bases onto the Joiner using the procedure explained in steps 7–9. You will need to pick up the modules as you assemble them. Adjust each Joiner flap to center it in the Base, then lock it in place. Keep the string loop free of the other bases.

11

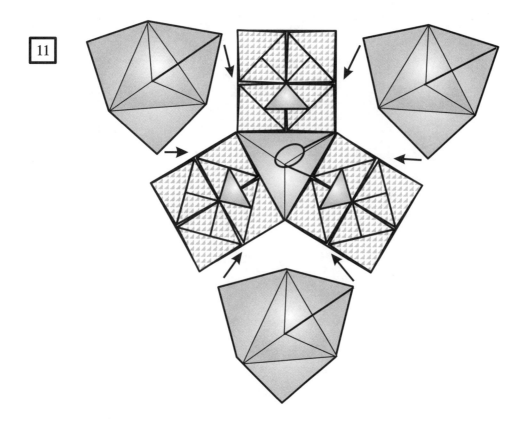

Add three more Concave Joiners to the assembly using the procedure explained in steps 7–9. You will need to hold the assembly as you add each Joiner. Each Joiner will have two flaps to insert and lock into the Bases. When you have joined the units together they will form a hollow bowl.

12

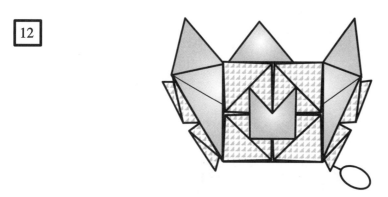

The result of step 11 is shown here. The Base shown in the following diagrams will be drawn from a distorted angle to show the internal flaps more clearly.

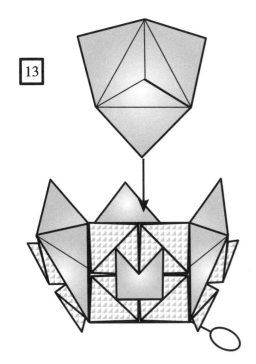

13

Add a Concave Joiner to one of the Bases on the bowl-shaped assembly.

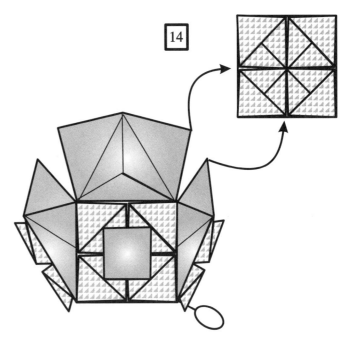

14

Add a Base to the assembly. Work your way around the bowl adding a Joiner, then a Base, until you have added three Joiners and three Bases. Step 15 shows how the model should look up to this point.

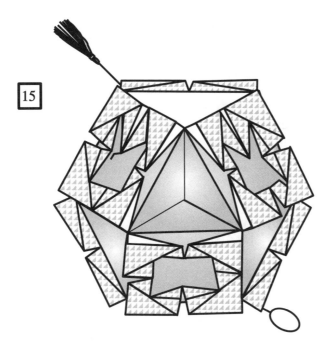

15

The model now has a total of six Bases, and seven Joiners. If you plan to add potpourri to the ball, you should do it now. If you plan to add a tassel, add it now.

16

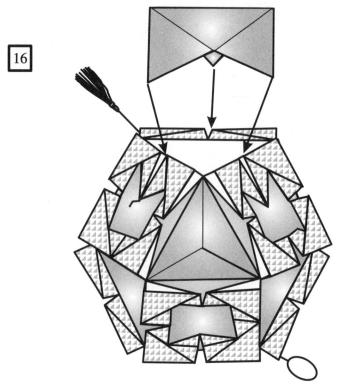

The last step is the most difficult. Lock each flap of the remaining Joiner to the assembly. You may find that it is easier to use a pair of tweezers to make the mountain fold, since it is no longer possible to reach the inside of the model. The flaps on the Joiner must remain on the outside of the assembly as each flap is locked into a Base.

17

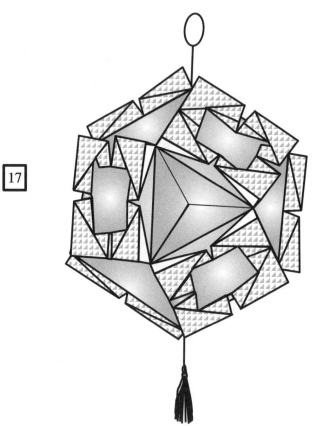

The Bases can be folded in different patterns, but the assembly of the ball (technically a Cuboctahedron) remains the same.

Wide-Pointed Star Ball

This ornament is made like the Ball Ornament but the Bases are folded differently. The ornament requires sixteen squares the same size. Fold six Bases; then, using foil or paper of a contrasting color, fold eight Concave Joiners and cut six Inserts for the Bases. Fold the Bases with the Inserts in place.

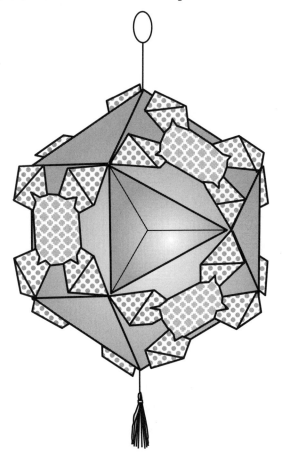

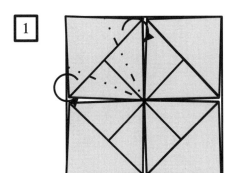

1. Begin with a Base. Mountain-fold the outer edges of the top near left flap in as far as they will go.

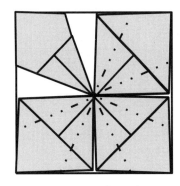

2. Repeat step 1 on the three remaining flaps.

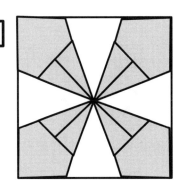

3. The finished folds will still allow a Joiner to be folded into the Base. Repeat these folds on the remaining five Bases. Follow the instructions for making a Ball Ornament on pages 46–50.

Four-Pointed Star Ball

This ornament is made like the Ball Ornament but the Bases are folded differently. The ornament requires sixteen squares the same size. Fold six Bases; then, using foil or paper of a contrasting color, fold eight Concave Joiners and and cut six Inserts for the Bases. Fold the Bases with the Inserts in place.

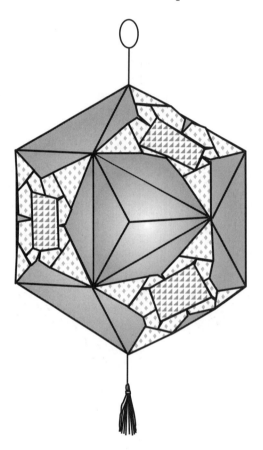

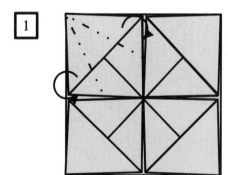

1 Begin with a Base. Mountain-fold the outer edges of the top near left flap in as far as they will go.

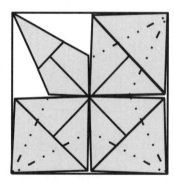

2 Repeat step 1 on the three remaining flaps.

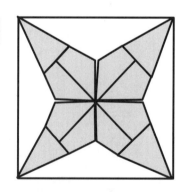

3 The finished folds will still allow a Joiner to be folded into the Base. Repeat these folds on the remaining five Bases. Follow the instructions for making a Ball Ornament on pages 46–50.

Cross Ball Ornament

This ornament requires sixteen squares the same size. Fold six Bases, then using foil or paper of a contrasting color, fold eight Concave Joiners and cut six Inserts for the Bases. Fold the Bases with the Inserts in place.

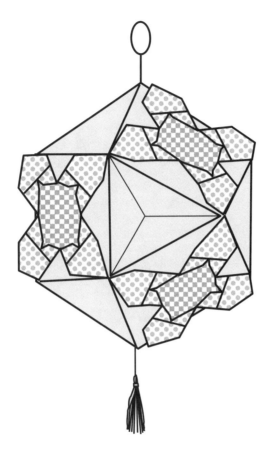

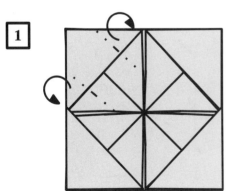

1

Begin with a Base. Mountain-fold the outer edges of the top near left flap in as far as they will go.

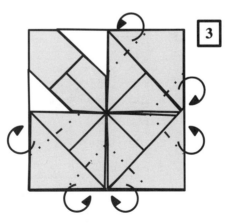

2

Repeat step 1 on the three remaining flaps.

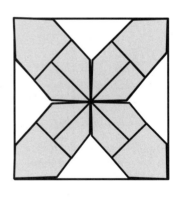

3

The finished folds will still allow a Joiner to be folded into the module. Repeat these folds on the remaining five Bases. Follow the instructions for making a Ball Ornament found on pages 46–50.

Star Flower Ball

This ornament takes sixteen squares of paper the same size. Fold six Bases. Then, using foil or a contrasting color, fold eight Joiners and six Inserts for the Bases. Fold the Bases with the Inserts in place.

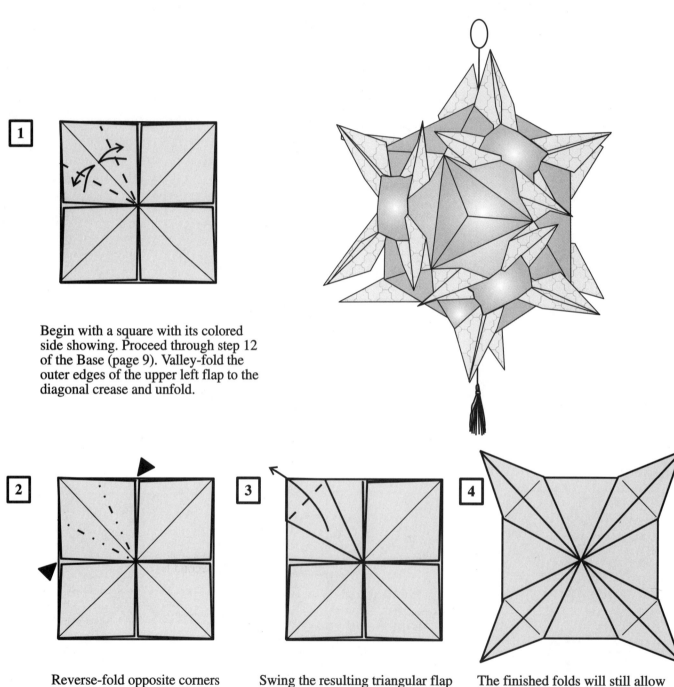

1

Begin with a square with its colored side showing. Proceed through step 12 of the Base (page 9). Valley-fold the outer edges of the upper left flap to the diagonal crease and unfold.

2

Reverse-fold opposite corners into the flap.

3

Swing the resulting triangular flap upward to the left as far as it will go and flatten. Repeat steps 1–3 on the three remaining flaps to form a Four-Pointed Star Base.

4

The finished folds will still allow a Joiner to be folded into the module. Repeat these folds on the five remaining Bases. Follow the instructions for making a Ball Ornament on pages 46–50.

Oddball

This ornament requires seventeen squares the same size. Fold six Bases; then, using foil or paper of a contrasting color, fold two Double Concave Joiners (instructions below), two Concave Joiners, three Hinges and cut six Inserts for the Bases. Fold the Bases with the Inserts in place.

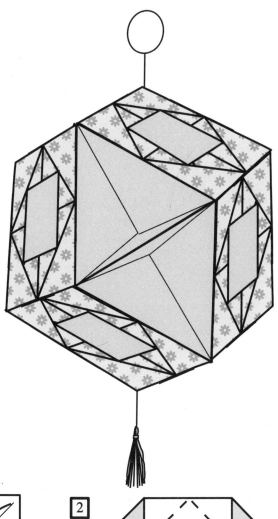

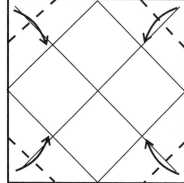

Begin with an unfolded Joiner. Valley-fold the corners to the crease formed in step 3 of the Joiner (page 13).

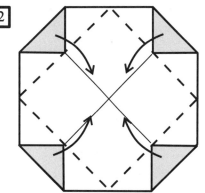

Valley-fold along the crease formed in step 3 of the Joiner.

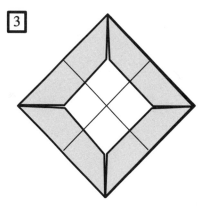

Repeat steps 1 and 2 on a second Joiner.

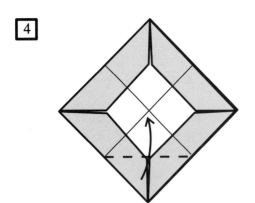

4

Valley-fold the bottom corner of one unit up to the center.

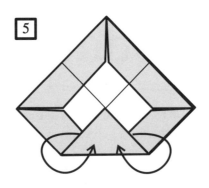

5

Gently pull out the inner flaps behind the near flap and lay them down on the near side of the unit.

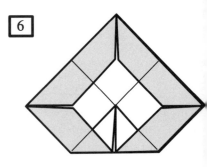

6

Step 5 has produced a pocket in the lower part of the Joiner.

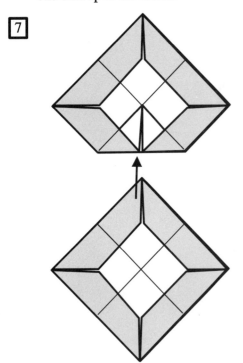

7

Insert the second Joiner into the pocket at the bottom of the first.

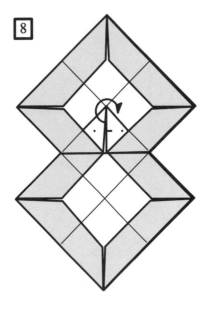

8

Lock the two Joiners.

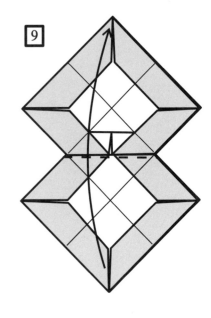

9

Valley-fold the Double Joiner upward in half.

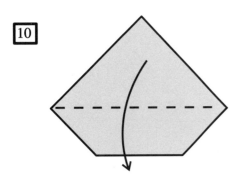

10

Valley-fold the top half of the near flap down.

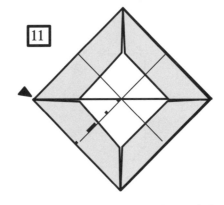

11

Reverse-fold downward the lower left portion of the near flap. (This is the same procedure used in forming a normal Joiner; see step 9 on page 14.)

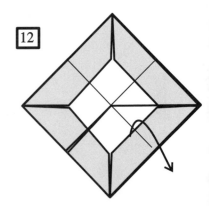

12

Open out the near right flap.

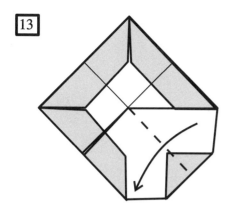

13

Valley-fold the near right flap downward.

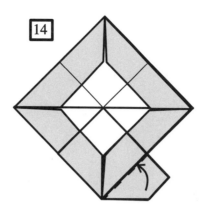

14

Valley-fold the small protruding flap up inside the Joiner.

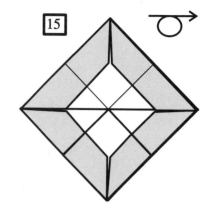

15

Turn the Joiner over.
Repeat steps 10 through 14.

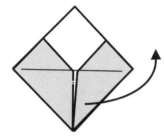

16

Enlarged view. Hold in place the farthest flap; grasp the bottom tip of the near flap and lift it forward and up. The unit will open into a pair of concave triangular bowls.

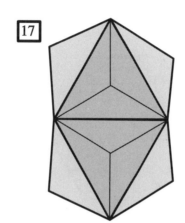

17

Enlarged View. The Double Concave Joiner can attach four Bases. Make two more Double Concave Joiners.

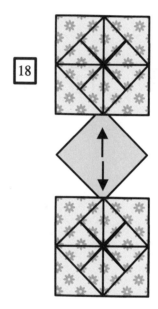

18

Join two Bases with a Hinge and lock in place.

19

Make a total of three assemblies.

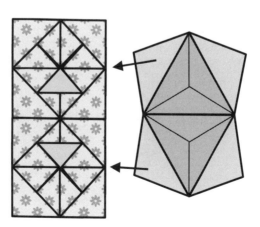

20

Join a Base assembly with a Double Concave Joiner. You will have to hold the two assemblies in your hands to accomplish this. The Joiner will remain bent as you insert and lock each side of the Base assembly.

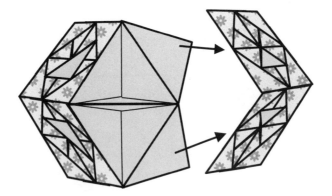

21

Continue building the Oddball by adding another
Base assembly to the Double Concave Joiner.

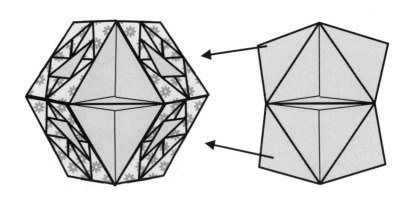

22

Lock a second Double Concave Joiner to the Base
assembly.

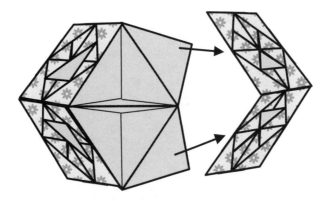

23

Continue by adding a third Base assembly
and one more Double Concave Joiner to
complete a ball open at the top and at the
bottom.

24

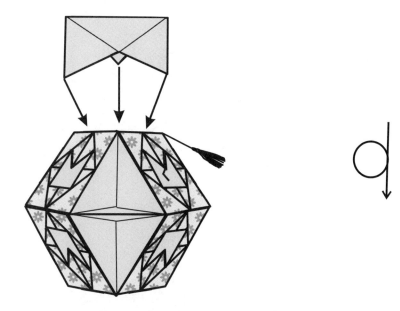

Add a tasseled string to one of the open base flaps; then insert and lock a Concave Joiner (pages 46 and 47) to the ball assembly. **Turn the open ball over** to continue with step 25.

25

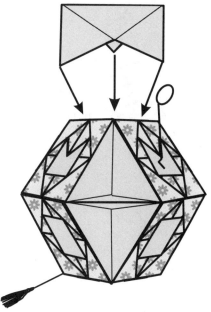

Add a looped string to one of the open Base flaps; then insert and lock a Concave Joiner to the ball assembly.

26

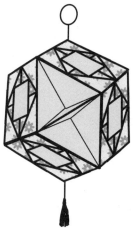

Disco Ball

This ornament requires thirty-six squares the same size. Fold eighteen Bases as for the Two-Dimensional Icon (page 23); then, using foil or paper of a contrasting color, fold eight Joiners and twenty Hinges. Cut eighteen Inserts for the Bases. Fold the Bases with the Inserts in place.

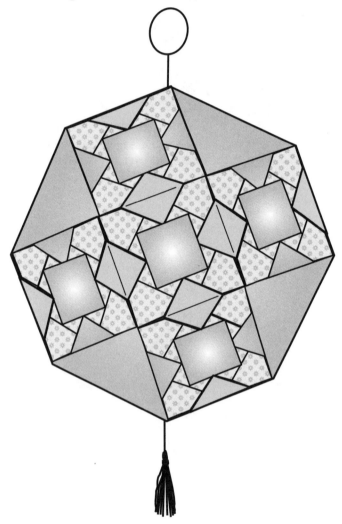

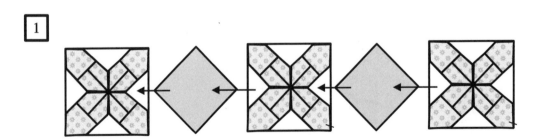

1

Begin by locking together eight Bases and seven Hinges.

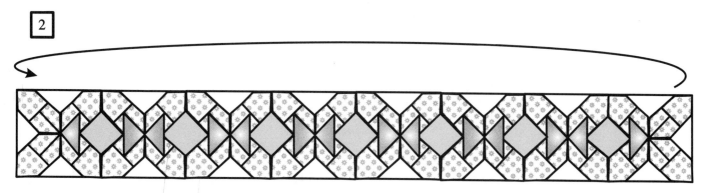

Swing the far right end backward to the left to form a circle.

3

Join the first and last Bases together with a Hinge and lock.

4

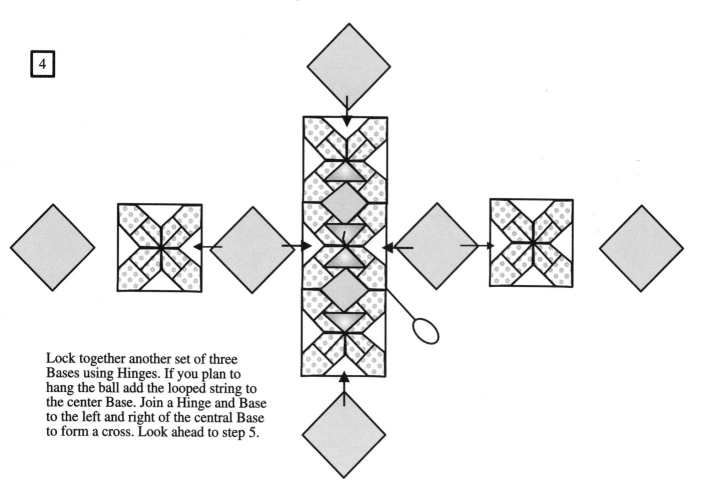

Lock together another set of three Bases using Hinges. If you plan to hang the ball add the looped string to the center Base. Join a Hinge and Base to the left and right of the central Base to form a cross. Look ahead to step 5.

5

Hold the Bases in
your hands and add
four Concave Joiners
to shape the assembly
into a bowl. You will
need to make two of
these assemblies
before you can
complete the ball. If
you want a tassel on
the bottom of the ball,
add the tassle string
to the center base of
the second assembly.
Keep the string loop
on the outside of the
assembly.

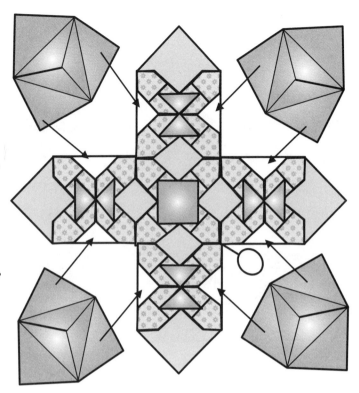

6

Lock the two bowl
assemblies to the
circle of Bases by
using Joiners and
Hinges.

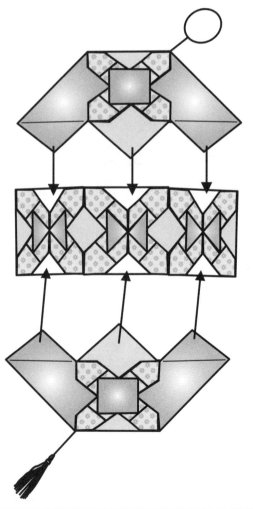

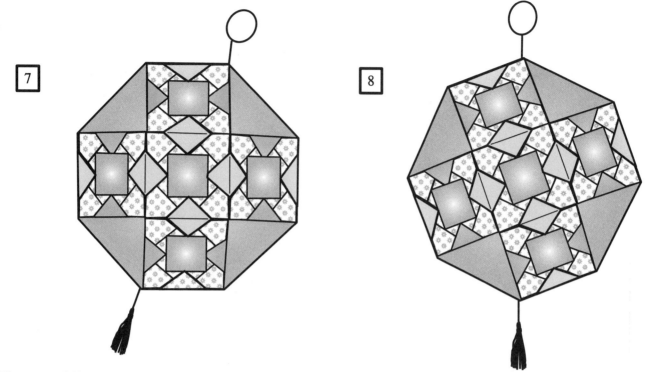

7
8

If you use foil Inserts and foil Joiners the ball will reflect light like a disco ball.

The Disco Ball, like many of the ornaments in this book, can be found in solid geometry. Polyhedrons are solid figures made up of flat surfaces joined together to form solids. The cube is a regular polyhedron. The balls are Cuboctahedrons. The Disco Ball is known as a Rhombicuboctahedron. The ornaments have added decorations through the use of Clips and folded Bases. Most of the standard polyhedrons can be made from the four models in this book. At some point you may wish to explore these possibilities in creating new ornaments.

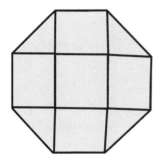

Rhombicuboctahedron

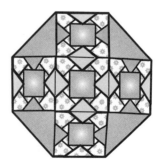

Disco Ball

Half-Dressed Cube

This ornament requires six squares of paper the same size. Fold three Three-Sided Bases (instructions below). Then, using foil or paper of a contrasting color, fold two Joiners and cut three Inserts for the Bases. Fold the Bases with the Inserts in place.

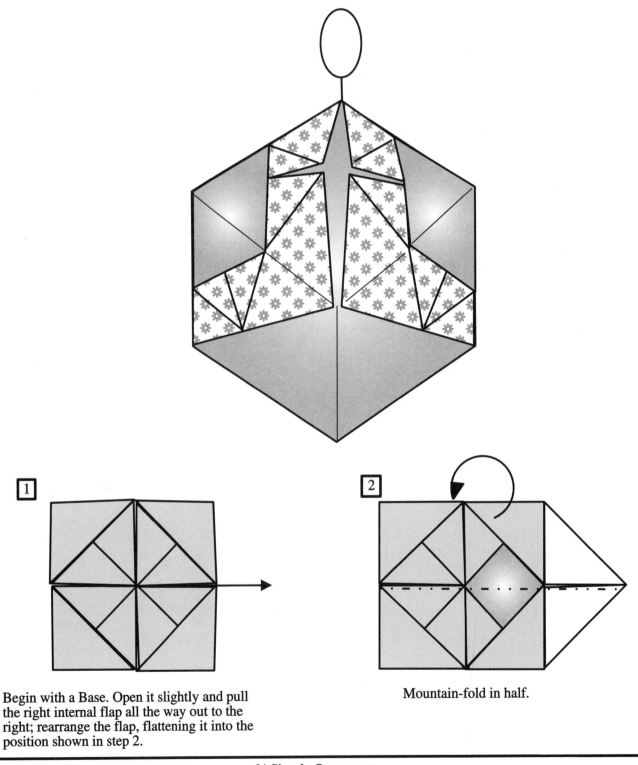

1

Begin with a Base. Open it slightly and pull the right internal flap all the way out to the right; rearrange the flap, flattening it into the position shown in step 2.

2

Mountain-fold in half.

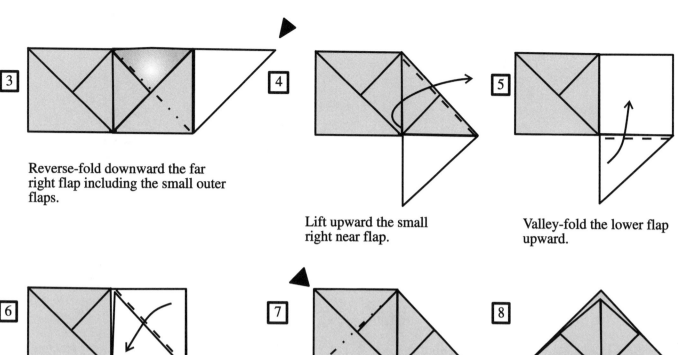

3 Reverse-fold downward the far right flap including the small outer flaps.

4 Lift upward the small right near flap.

5 Valley-fold the lower flap upward.

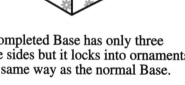

6 Fold back downward the top right portion of the flap lifted in step 4.

7 Reverse-fold inward the top left corners, handling them as a single corner.

8 Open out the unit from beneath into the shape of a triangular pyramid.

9 The completed Base has only three visible sides but it locks into ornaments in the same way as the normal Base.

Whenever possible, insert a flap from the Hinge or Joiner you are using into the side of the Three-Sided Base folded in steps 5–6. Lock this side of the Three-Sided Base first. The Bases can then be assembled into the ornament much more easily.

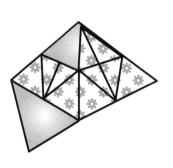

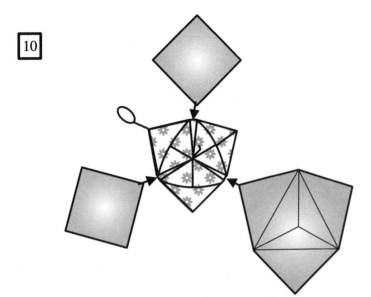

10

Begin assembling the cube by inserting two Hinges and a Joiner onto a Three-Sided Base and locking them. A looped string can be added to the Base for hanging the ornament.

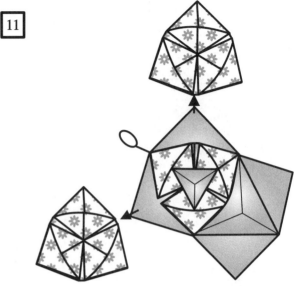

11

Lock down two Three-Sided Bases onto the Hinges of the assembly.

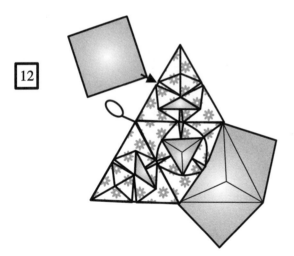

12

Insert a Hinge into the upper Three-Sided Base and lock it in place.

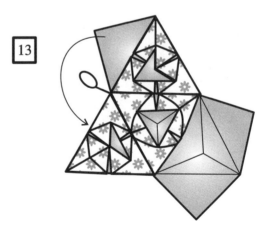

13

Hold the Ornament in your hands and form it into a cube. With the looped string on the outside, insert and lock the free flap of the Hinge into the adjoining Three-Sided Base.

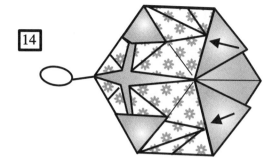

14

Lock one of the Joiner flaps into the Three-Sided Base.
Repeat with the remaining Joiner flap.

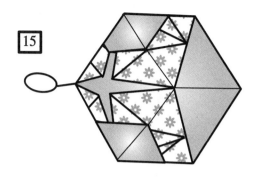

15

The Half-Dressed Cube is ready to hang.

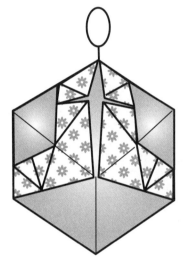

16

You can attach a tassel to the ornament by folding
the Joiner using the instructions for the Magic
Cube (page 43). This does not change the way the
ornament is assembled.

Fully Dressed Cube

This ornament requires seven squares of paper the same size. Fold four Three-Sided Bases (pages 64 and 65). Then, using foil or paper of a contrasting color, fold six Hinges and cut four Inserts for the Bases. Fold the Bases with the Inserts in place.

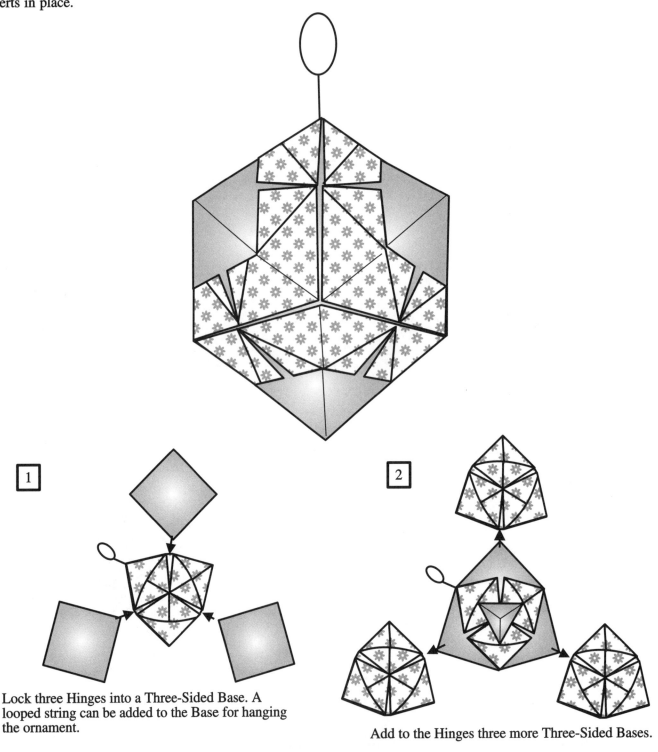

1

Lock three Hinges into a Three-Sided Base. A looped string can be added to the Base for hanging the ornament.

2

Add to the Hinges three more Three-Sided Bases.

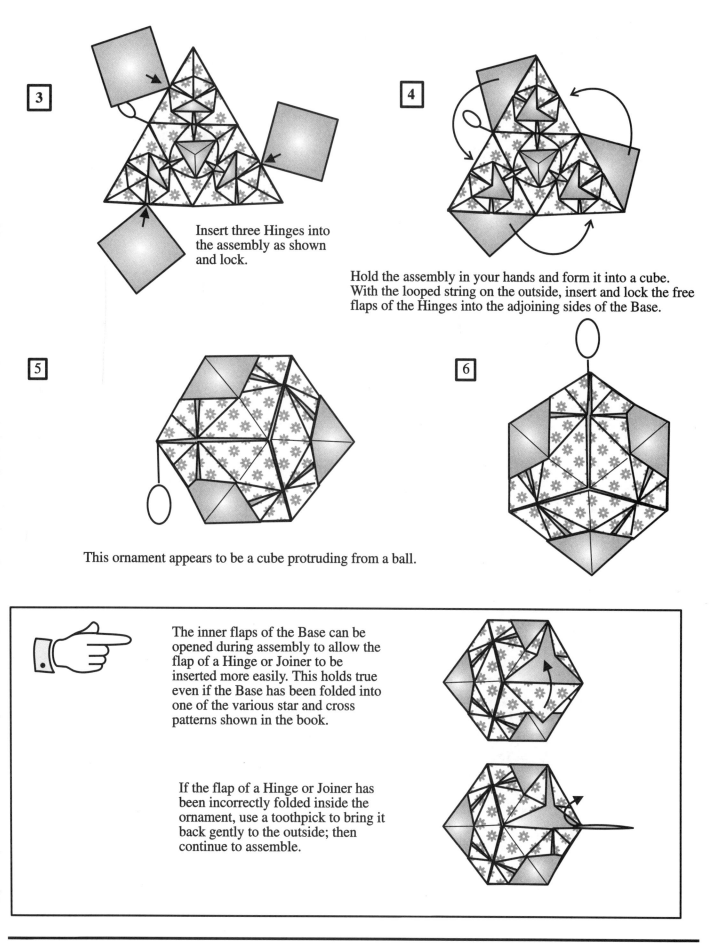

3

Insert three Hinges into the assembly as shown and lock.

4

Hold the assembly in your hands and form it into a cube. With the looped string on the outside, insert and lock the free flaps of the Hinges into the adjoining sides of the Base.

5

This ornament appears to be a cube protruding from a ball.

6

The inner flaps of the Base can be opened during assembly to allow the flap of a Hinge or Joiner to be inserted more easily. This holds true even if the Base has been folded into one of the various star and cross patterns shown in the book.

If the flap of a Hinge or Joiner has been incorrectly folded inside the ornament, use a toothpick to bring it back gently to the outside; then continue to assemble.

Siamese Cube

This ornament requires ten squares of paper the same size. Fold six Three-Sided Bases (pages 64 and 65). Then, using foil or paper of a contrasting color, fold nine Hinges and cut six Inserts for the Bases. Fold the Bases with the Inserts in place.

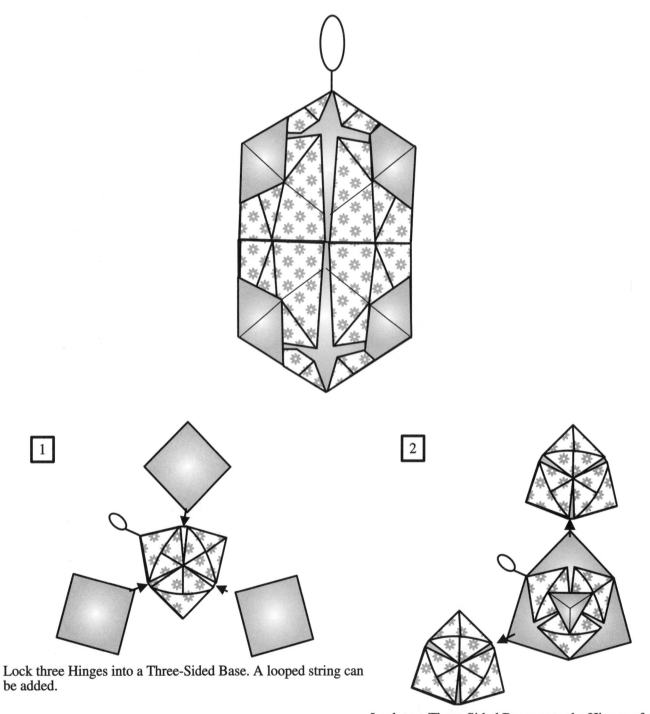

1

Lock three Hinges into a Three-Sided Base. A looped string can be added.

2

Lock two Three-Sided Bases onto the Hinges of the assembly.

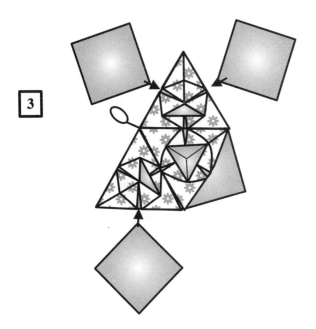

3

Lock three Hinges into the assembly.

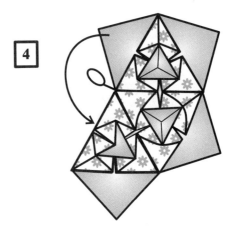

4

Hold the ornament in your hands and form it into an open-ended cube. Lock the indicated Hinge into the adjoining Three-Sided Base.

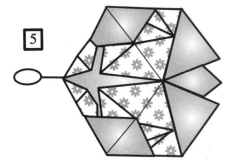

5

This completes half of the Siamese Cube.

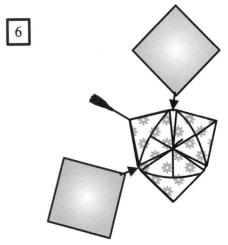

6

Insert two Hinges into a Three-Sided Base and lock. You may add a string tassel to the Base.

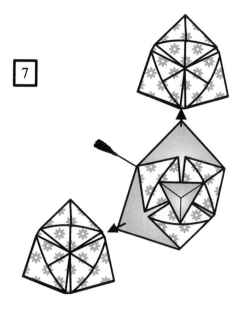

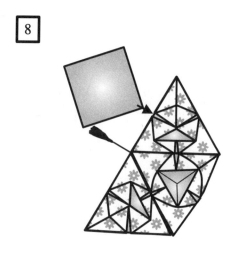

7

Lock two Three-Sided Bases to the Hinges of the assembly.

8

Insert a Hinge and lock.

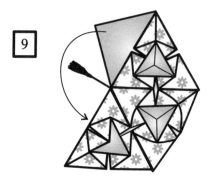

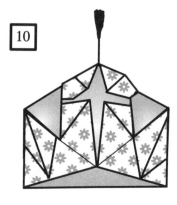

9

Hold the assembly in your hands and form it into an open cube. Insert the free Hinge into the adjoining Three-Sided Base and lock.

10

This completed second half of the Siamese Cube has the pockets necessary to join the two parts.

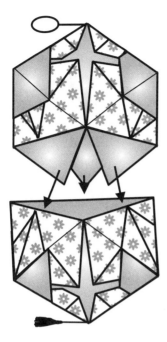

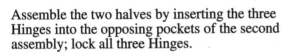

Assemble the two halves by inserting the three Hinges into the opposing pockets of the second assembly; lock all three Hinges.

The completed ornament looks like two cubes joined together.

Orb

This ornament requires thirteen squares of paper the same size. Fold eight Three-sided Bases. Then, using foil or paper of a contrasting color, fold twelve Hinges and cut eight Inserts for the Bases. Fold the Bases with the Inserts in place.

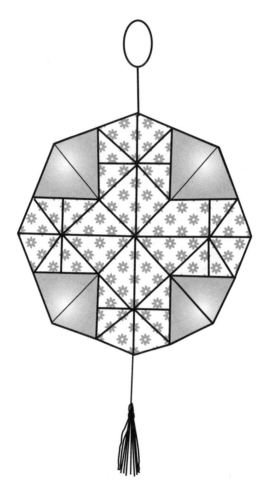

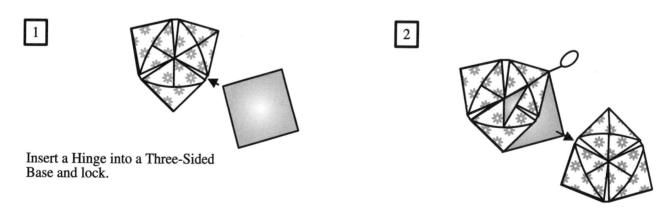

1 Insert a Hinge into a Three-Sided Base and lock.

2 Add a Three-Sided Base to the Hinge and lock. Add a looped string before locking.

3

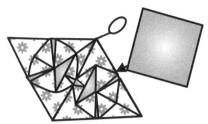

Insert a Hinge into the second
Three-Sided Base and lock.

4

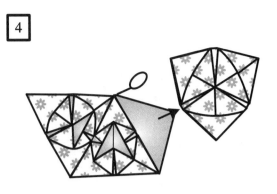

Add a third Three-Sided Base to the Hinge and
lock.

5

Insert a Hinge into the third Three-Sided Base and lock.

6

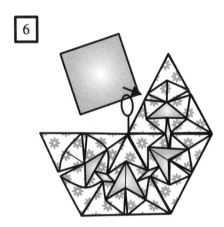

Add a fourth Three-Sided Base and another Hinge.

7

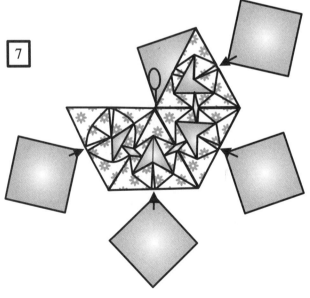

Insert four more Hinges and lock.

8

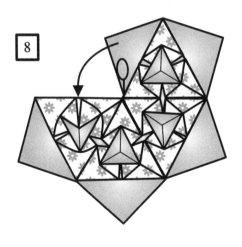

Hold the assembly in your hands and form it into a
bowl shape. Insert a Hinge into the adjoining Base as
indicated and lock.

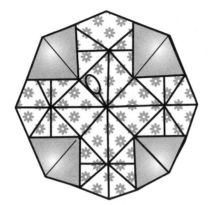
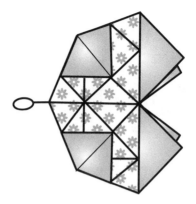

Top and side view of the completed step 8.

10

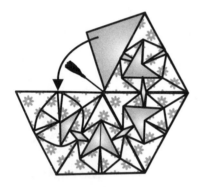

Repeat steps 1–6 to begin the second half of the Orb. Hold the assembly in your hands and form it into a bowl. You may wish to add a tassel string to this second half. Insert and lock the Hinge.

11

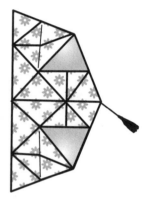

The second half has the pockets necessary to complete the ornament.

12

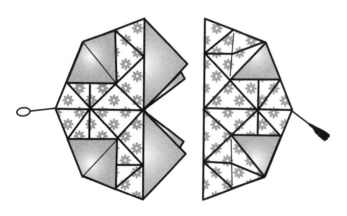

Join the two halves of the Orb by inserting the Hinges into the opposing pockets of the second half and locking them.

13

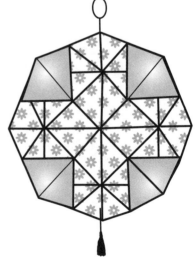

The Orb has the appearance of a perfect ball.

Tristar

This ornament requires six squares of paper the same size. Fold two Three-Sided Bases (page 64). Then, using foil or paper of a contrasting color, fold three Tristar Clips (instructions on this page); cut two Inserts. Fold the Bases with the Inserts in place.

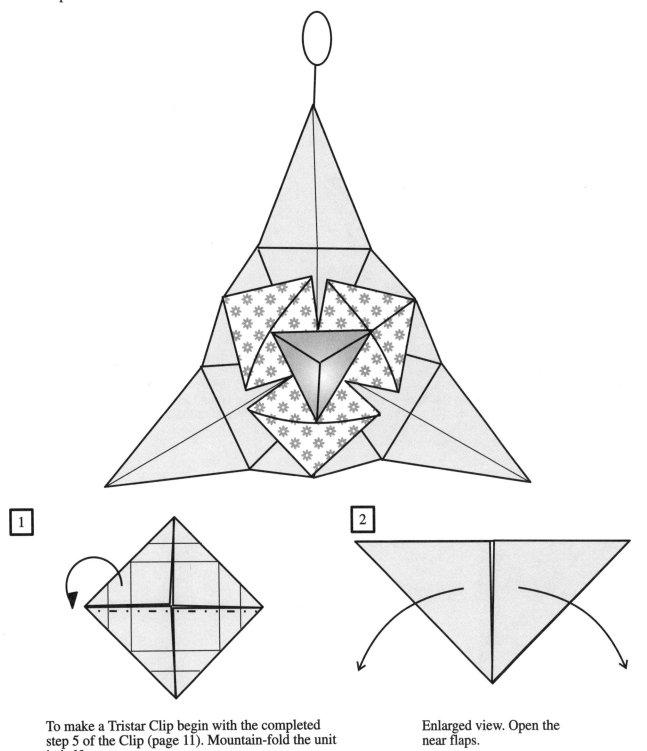

1 To make a Tristar Clip begin with the completed step 5 of the Clip (page 11). Mountain-fold the unit in half.

2 Enlarged view. Open the near flaps.

3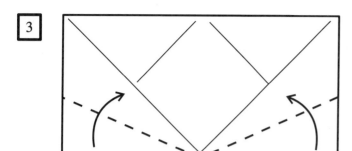

Valley-fold the right and left bottom edges up to the crease lines.

4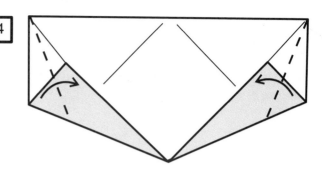

Valley-fold the outer edges to the crease lines.

5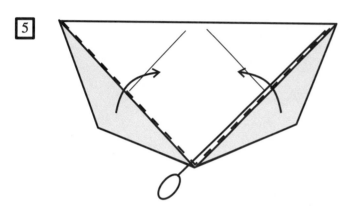

If you are going to hang an ornament using this Clip insert the string directly under one of the near flaps and continue to fold the Clip with the string in place. You will need only one string per ornament. Valley-fold the near flaps up along the existing crease lines.

6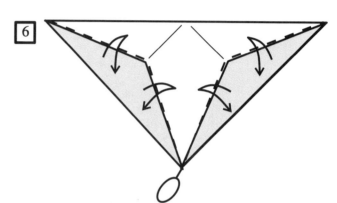

Valley-fold the near half of the unit along the inner edges of the near flaps and unfold.

7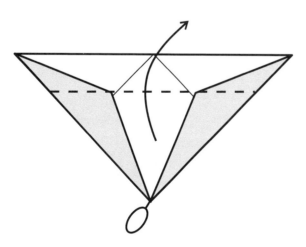

Valley-fold the entire lower portion of the near flap upward as shown.

8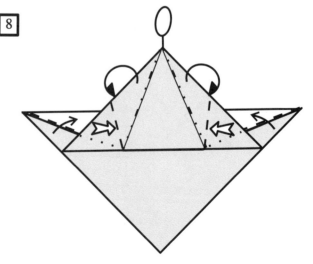

Swing the edges of the flap inward along the creases formed in step 6. Look ahead to step 9.

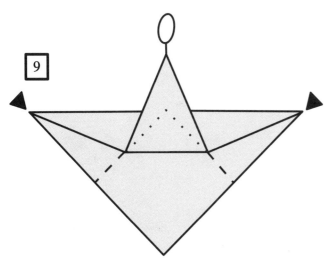

9

Reverse-fold the outer points downward; the creases on the far half of the unit already exist.

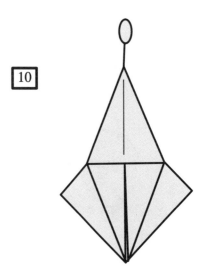

10

The two near flaps should be folded as one when the Tristar Clip is being locked into the ornament.

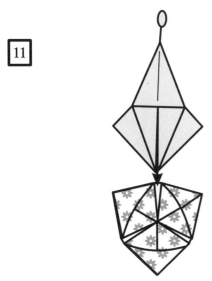

11

Begin assembling the Tristar by inserting the two adjoining flaps of the Tristar Clip into the pocket of a Three-Sided Base; lock.

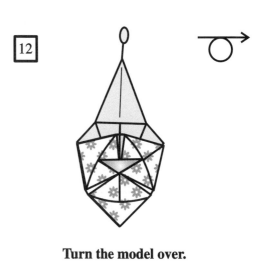

12

Turn the model over.

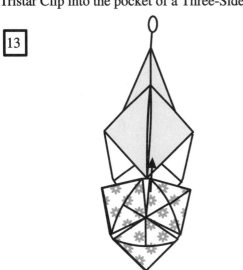

13

Join a second Three-Sided Base onto the Tristar Clip and lock.

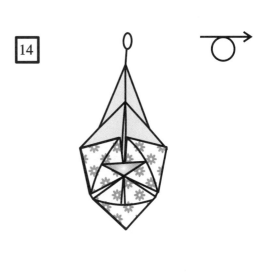

14

Turn the model over.

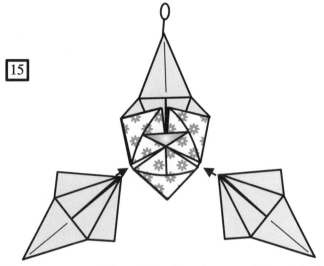

15

Insert two more Tristar Clips into the assembly and lock them into place both in front and behind.

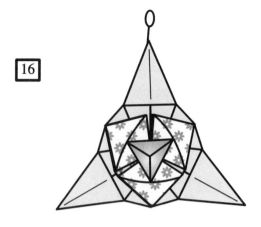

16

The completed Tristar Ornament looks much like a three-petaled flower.

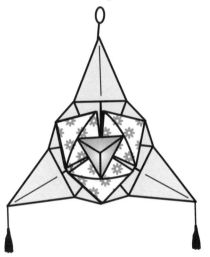

The Tristar Ornament with two added string tassels.

Locking the Clip onto the Three-Sided Base is one of the hardest maneuvers in this book. A pair of tweezers or a popsicle stick may help. Place the stick on top of the flaps you are going to lock together. Using a twisting motion rock the two flaps down into the pocket and then crease them in place. The creases already exist, and this makes a tricky procedure somewhat less difficult.

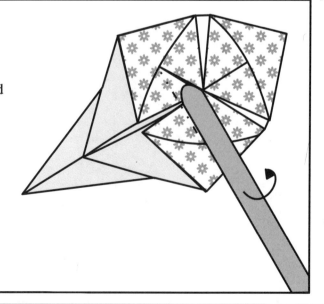

Baffled Lantern

This ornament requires eleven squares of paper the same size. Fold three Bases. Then, using foil or paper of a contrasting color, fold three Two-Color Clips, two Two-Colored Joiners (intructions for both are found below), and cut eight Inserts for the Bases. Fold the Clips, Joiners, and Bases with the Inserts in place.

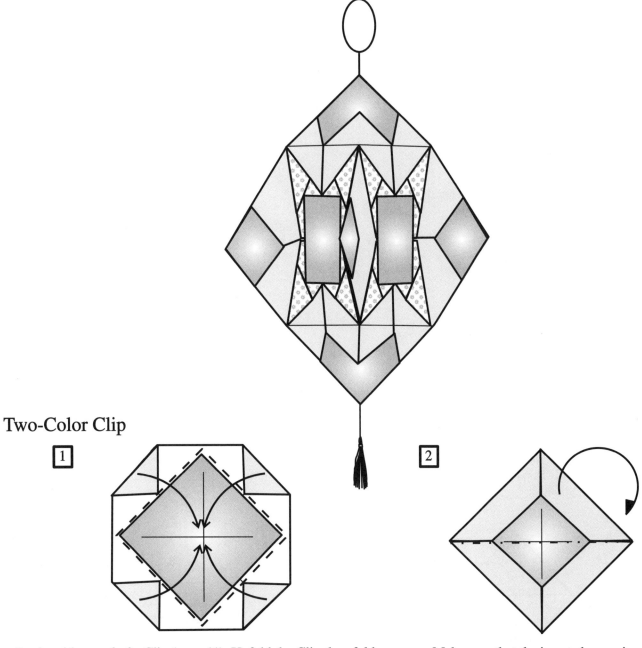

Two-Color Clip

1

Begin with step 6 of a Clip (page 11). Unfold the Clip then fold the corners in to the creases formed in step 3 on page 11. Place an Insert of foil or contrasting color paper in the very center of the Clip. Using existing creases, fold the outer blunt corners inward over the inserted square.

2

Make sure that the inserted paper is centered and then mountain-fold the model in half.

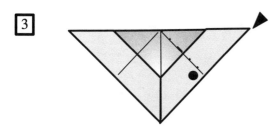

3

Reverse-fold the top right corner downward; the creases already exist. Watch the black dot.

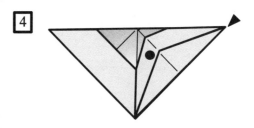

4

The action of step 3 is shown here in progress.

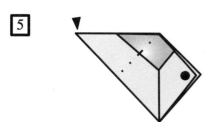

5

Reverse-fold the left corner downward.

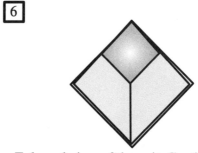

6

Enlarged view of the unit. Continue with steps 12 through 17 of the Clip (page 12). This completes the Two-Color Clip.

Two-Color Joiner

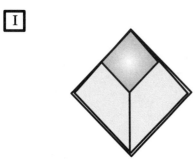

I

Begin making the Two-Color Joiner by repeating only steps 1 through 5 for the Two-Color Clip.

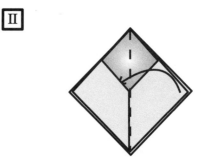

II

Tuck the near right flap into the pocket of the near left flap.

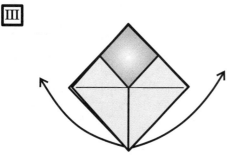

III

Open the unit from beneath to complete the Two-Color Joiner.

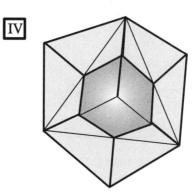

IV

The Two-Color Joiner as seen from the top. The Insert is now visible in the central portion.

Baffled Lantern

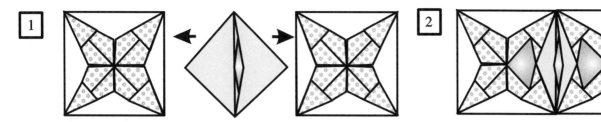

1 Insert the flaps of a Two-Color Clip into the sides of two Bases and lock. The illustration shows a Base folded into a Star Pattern (page 37), but you may fold it into any pattern you wish.

2 If you have included an insert in the Base, it will begin to show as you lock the different parts together.

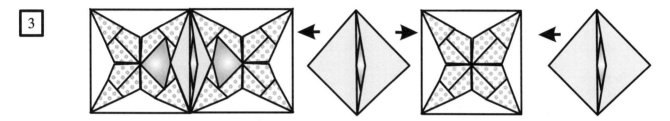

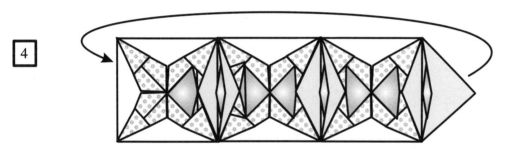

3 Fasten to the assembly another Two-Color Clip and another Base. Then insert a third Two-Color Clip into the last Base and lock.

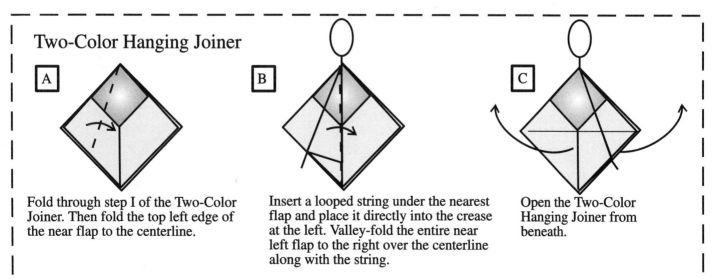

4 Swing the far right end of the assembly backward to the left; insert the right flap into the left pocket and lock.

Two-Color Hanging Joiner

A Fold through step I of the Two-Color Joiner. Then fold the top left edge of the near flap to the centerline.

B Insert a looped string under the nearest flap and place it directly into the crease at the left. Valley-fold the entire near left flap to the right over the centerline along with the string.

C Open the Two-Color Hanging Joiner from beneath.

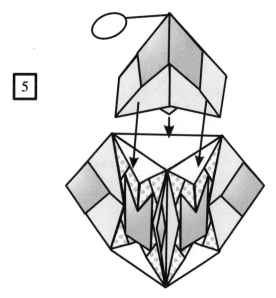

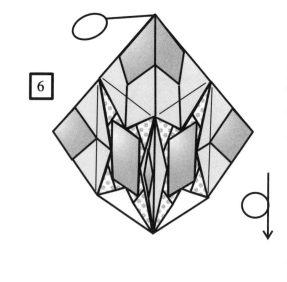

Insert the three flaps of the Two-Color
Hanging Joiner (from step C on page
83) into the base ring and lock.

Turn the ornament over.

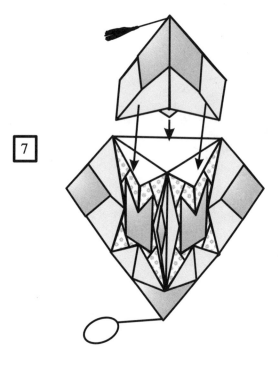

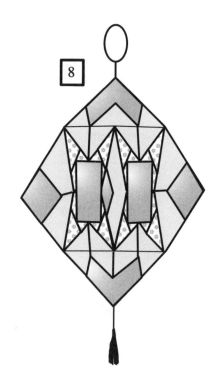

Repeat steps I–IV on page 82 to make the bottom of
the lantern. If you want to add a tassel string to the
ornament, add this in the same way as the looped
string, in steps A–C on page 83.

Lantern

This ornament requires eight squares of paper the same size. Fold three Bases. Then, using foil or paper of a contrasting color, fold two Hinges and two Joiners.

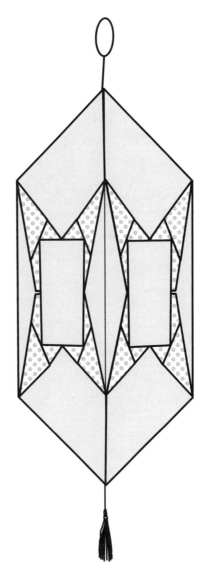

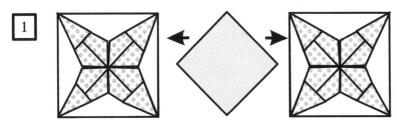

Insert a Hinge into the sides of two Bases and lock. The illustration shows a Base folded into a Star Pattern (page 37), but you may fold it into any pattern you wish.

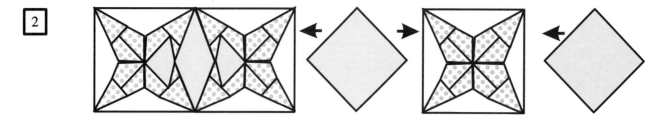

2

Fasten to the assembly another Hinge and another Base. Then insert a third Hinge into the last Base and lock.

3

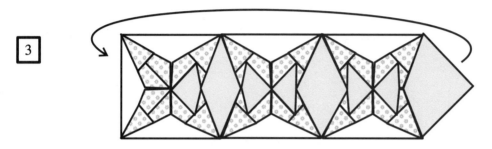

Swing the far right end of the assembly backward to the left; insert the right flap into the left pocket and lock to form an open three-sided ring.

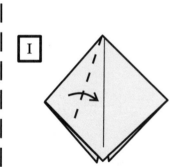

I

If you are going to use a looped string, make a Hanging Joiner. Begin with step 12 of the Clip (page 12). Then valley-fold the top left edge of the near flap to the centerline.

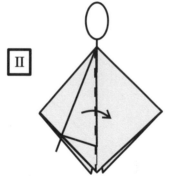

II

Insert a looped string under the nearest flap and place it directly into the crease at the left. Valley-fold the entire near left flap (with the string) to the right over the centerline.

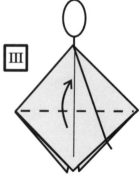

III

Valley-fold the bottom corner of the near flap up to the top corner.

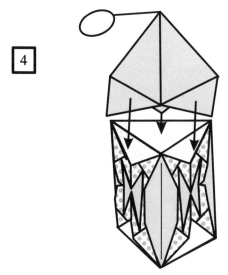

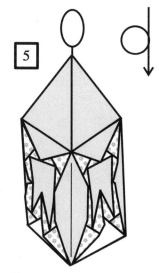

Insert the three flaps of the Hanging Joiner into the base ring and lock.

Turn the ornament over.

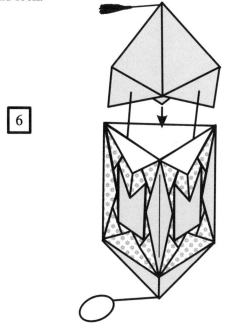

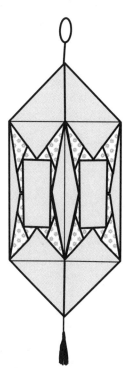

Repeat steps I through III to make the bottom of the Lantern. If you want to add a tassel string to the ornament, add it in the same way as the looped string.

Four-Sided Carousel

This ornament requires fourteen squares the same size. Fold four Bases. Then, using foil or paper of a contrasting color, fold eight Tandem Joiners (instructions below), four Hinges, and cut four Inserts for the Bases. Fold the Bases with the Inserts in place.

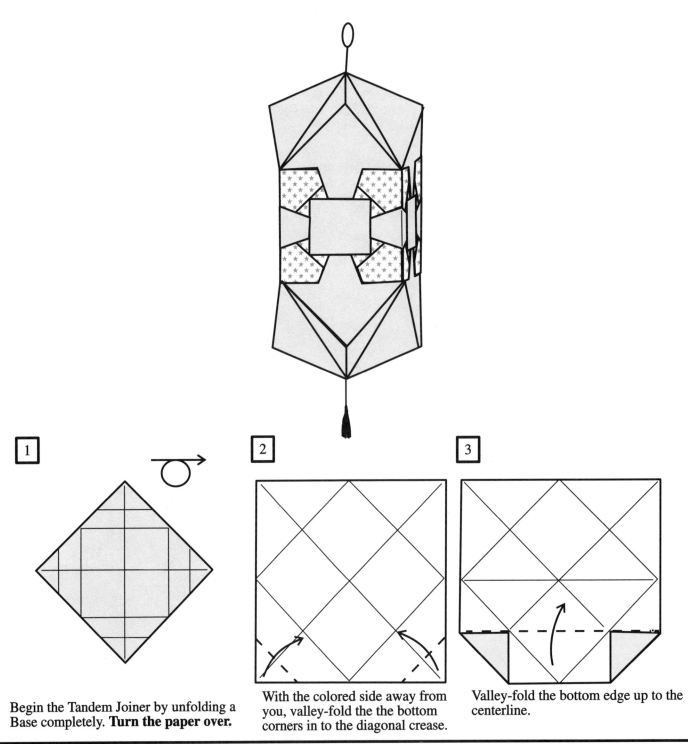

1

Begin the Tandem Joiner by unfolding a Base completely. **Turn the paper over.**

2

With the colored side away from you, valley-fold the the bottom corners in to the diagonal crease.

3

Valley-fold the bottom edge up to the centerline.

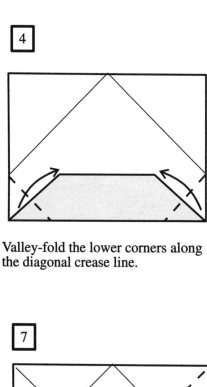

4

Valley-fold the lower corners along the diagonal crease line.

5

Return the lower corners to their former position.

6

Swivel the upper left corner of the near flap to the exact center of the bottom edge; watch the black dots. Repeat with the upper right corner of the rear flap.

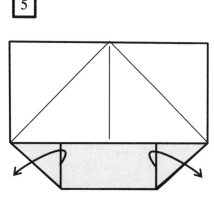

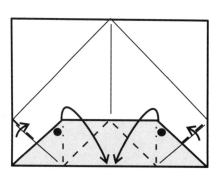

7

Valley-fold the unit in half along the diagonal.

8

Reverse-fold the top right corner to the left.

9

Open the near right flap slightly toward the right; then valley-fold the top left flaps as one down into the large pocket just opened.

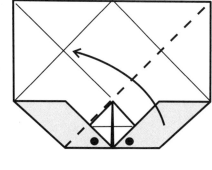

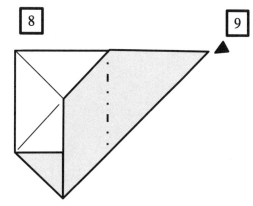

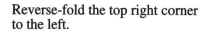

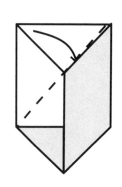

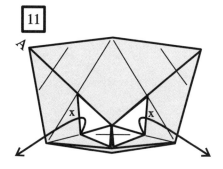

10

Pull the nearest top central corner clockwise down to the right to open the Joiner. Adjust the Joiner into the position shown in step 11.

11

The Tandem Joiner is now three-dimensional. It is shaped like the inner corner of a box: think of this as the *box* shape. The lower colored layers form pockets; pull these pockets into a vertical, or open, position. Watch the spots marked X.

12

The Tandem Joiner, now in open position, has been opened into the shape of an irregular bowl: think of this as the *bowl* shape. Fold a total of eight Tandem Joiners.

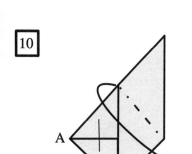

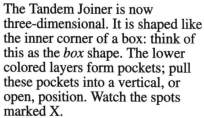

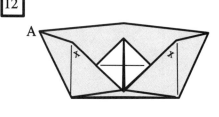

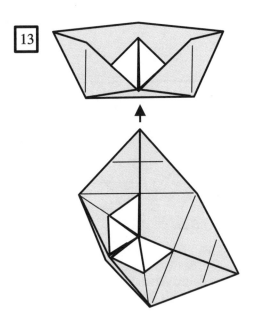

13

The Joiner at the top is in the *bowl* shape. Insert the corner of a second, *box*-shaped, Joiner into the bottom front pocket of the first. (Insert the double-layer corner—the thinner of the two corners—into this pocket.)

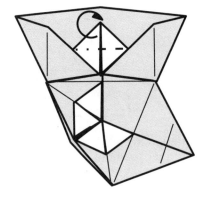

Lock.

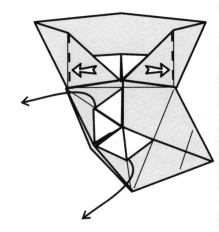

Return the upper Joiner to *box* shape. Open the lower Joiner into a *bowl* shape.

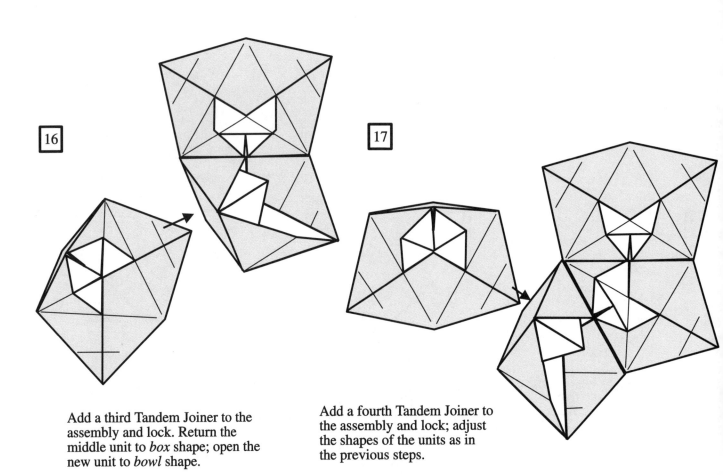

16

Add a third Tandem Joiner to the assembly and lock. Return the middle unit to *box* shape; open the new unit to *bowl* shape.

17

Add a fourth Tandem Joiner to the assembly and lock; adjust the shapes of the units as in the previous steps.

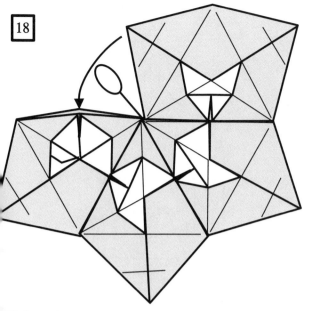

18

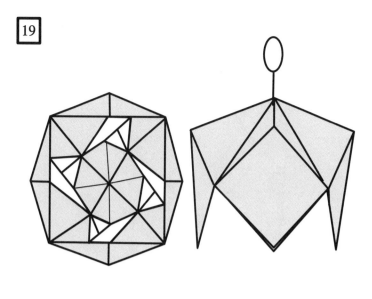

19

Pick up the assembly and hold it in your hands. Shape the assembly into a concave form, and lock the remaining flap from the fourth Joiner to the first Joiner. If you intend to hang your ornament, insert a looped string before locking the final flap.

Step 5 shows the interior of the assembly and a side view. Make a second Tandem Joiner Assembly. If you want to have a tassel on the ornament, add it before locking down the last flap.

20

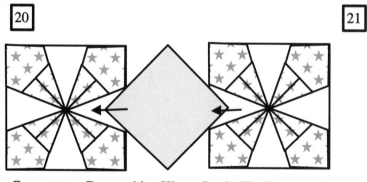

21

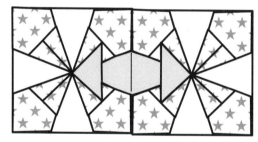

Connect two Bases with a Hinge. Lock. The Bases are in Wide-Pointed Star form (page 51).

Join two more Bases and lock. Join the four Bases using a third Hinge. Add an extra Hinge on the fourth base. This is the same procedure as with the Cube.

22

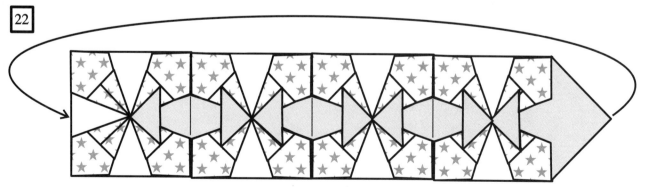

Swing the far right end of the assembly backward to the left; insert and lock the right Hinge into the left Base, completing an open box.

23

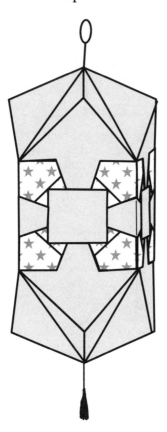

Insert and lock the four flaps of the Tandem Joiner assembly into the pockets of the open box.

24

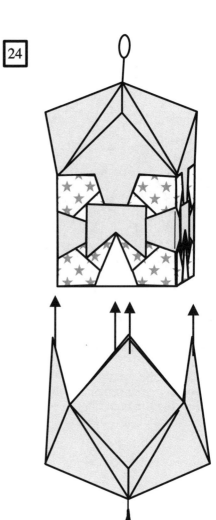

Insert and lock the second Tandem Joiner assembly onto the box to complete the Four-Sided Carousel.

25

Five-Sided Carousel

This ornament requires eighteen squares of paper the same size. Fold five Bases. Then, using foil or paper of a contrasting color, fold five Hinges, ten Tandem Joiners, and cut five Inserts for the Bases. Fold the Bases with the Inserts in place.

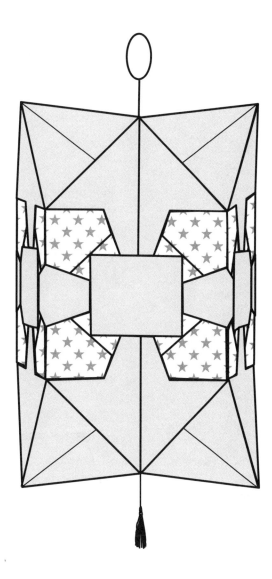

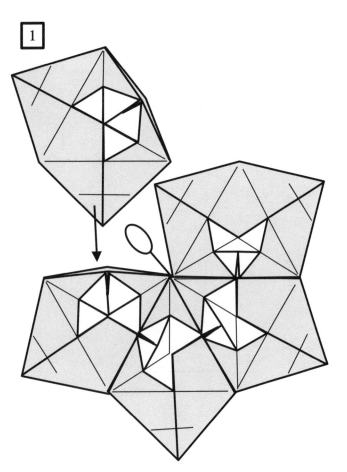

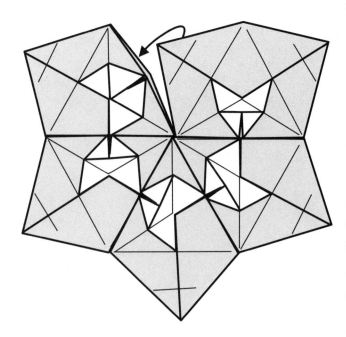

2

Pick up the assembly and hold it in your hands. Shape the assembly into a concave bowl, and lock the flap of the fifth Joiner to the first. If you intend to hang your ornament, insert a looped string before locking the final flap.

Proceed through step 17 of the Four-Sided Carousel. Insert the flap from a fifth Tandem Joiner into the pocket of the Four-Sided Carousel assembly and lock. (Use the double-layer flap for assembly.)

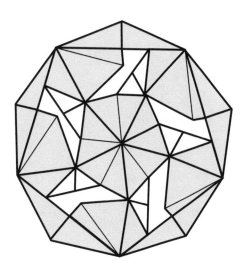

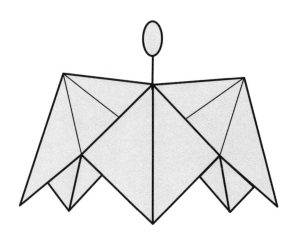

3

Step 3 shows the interior of the assembly and a side view. Make a second Tandem Joiner assembly. If you want to have a tassel, add it before locking the last flap.

4

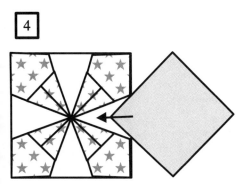

Insert a Hinge into a Base and lock.

5

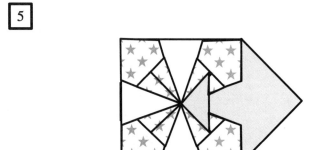

Make a four-sided chain and add to the end, the assembly made in step 4, making a five-sided chain.

6

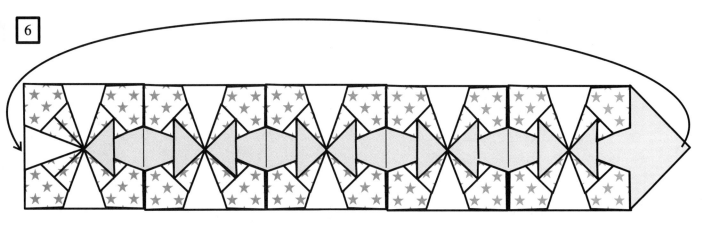

Swing the right end backward to the left; insert and lock the right Hinge into the left Base, making a five-sided ring.

7

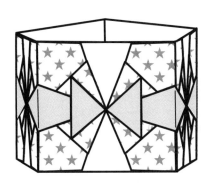

The five-sided ring.

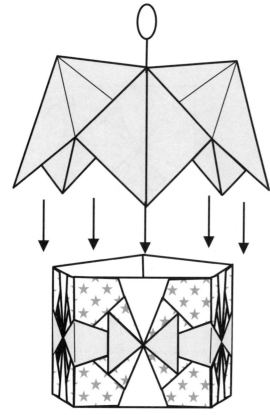

Insert and lock the five flaps of the
Tandem Joiner assembly into the
pockets of the five-sided ring.

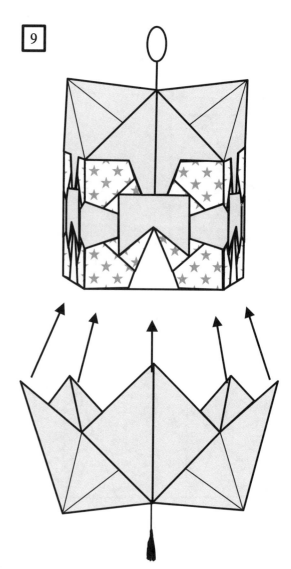

Insert and lock the second Tandem
Joiner assembly onto the five-sided ring
to complete the Five-Sided Carousel.

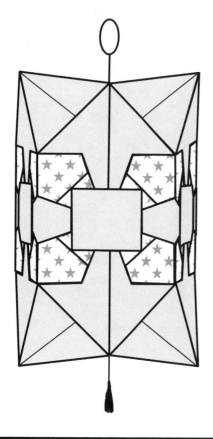

Complex Ornaments

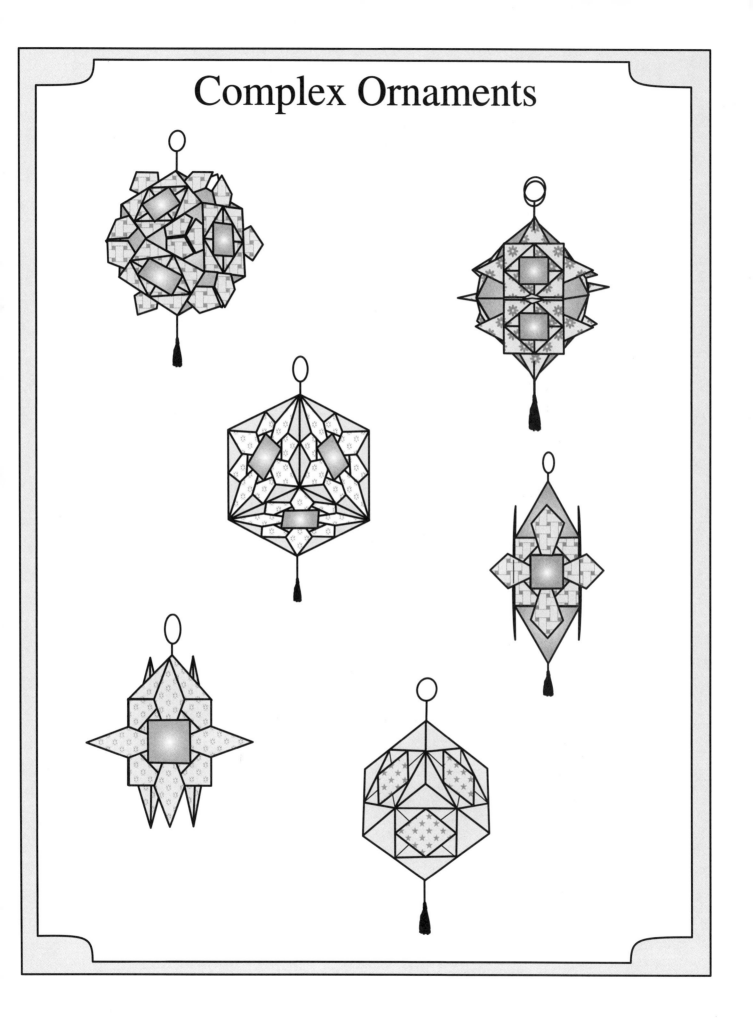

Complex Ornaments Procedures

It is necessary to change the size of paper to make the Complex Bases found in this section of the book. Only the Complex Bases need larger squares of paper. These can easily be made by following the instructions below. Remember that only the Complex Bases need to have the larger squares of paper; all other units remain the same size as the Simple Ornaments.

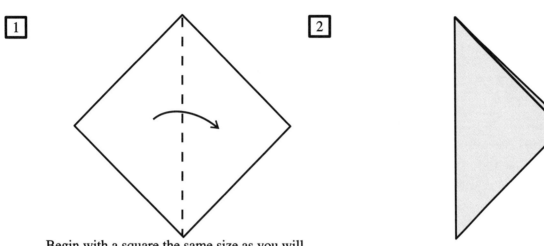

1	2

Begin with a square the same size as you will use for the Clips and Joiners. Valley-fold the square in half diagonally.

Crease the folded edge hard.

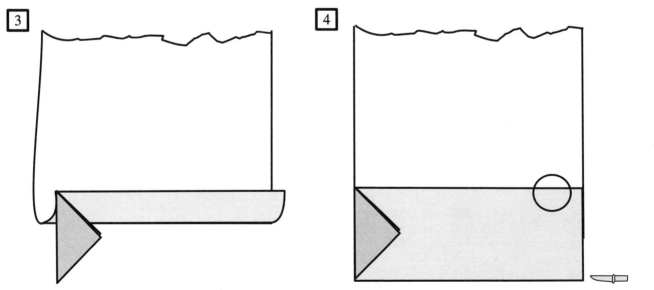

3

4

Begin making a large square of paper by starting with step 4 on page 3. Hold together as shown the folded triangle (from step 2 above) and the lower left corner of the Christmas gift wrap. Move both upward until the bottom tip of the triangle meets the bottom edge of the gift wrap.

Hold down the two layers of paper and carefully cut away the near layer using a plastic picnic knife or letter opener. Make the cut as straight as possible along the new crease.

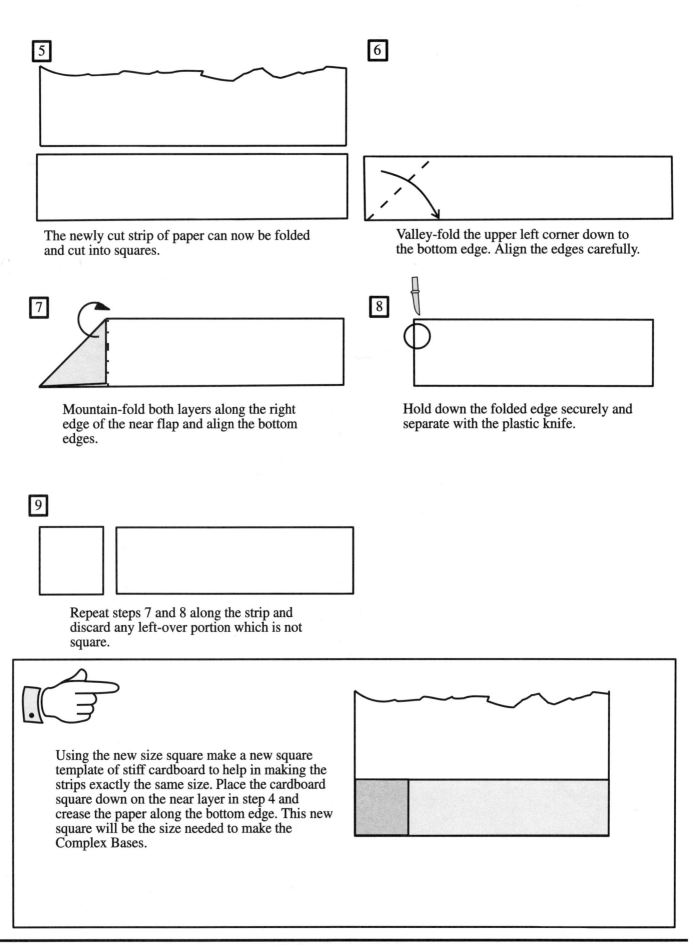

5

The newly cut strip of paper can now be folded
and cut into squares.

6

Valley-fold the upper left corner down to
the bottom edge. Align the edges carefully.

7

Mountain-fold both layers along the right
edge of the near flap and align the bottom
edges.

8

Hold down the folded edge securely and
separate with the plastic knife.

9

Repeat steps 7 and 8 along the strip and
discard any left-over portion which is not
square.

Using the new size square make a new square
template of stiff cardboard to help in making the
strips exactly the same size. Place the cardboard
square down on the near layer in step 4 and
crease the paper along the bottom edge. This new
square will be the size needed to make the
Complex Bases.

Complex Base

All of the ornaments in this section require that the Complex Base remain blintz folded. The folding is exactly the same as the Base for the Simple Ornaments except that the paper is not completely unfolded in the last steps.

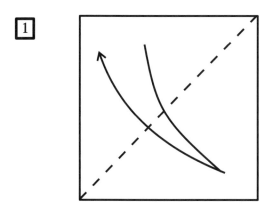

Begin with the larger square of paper needed for the Complex Base. Valley-fold along the diagonal and unfold.

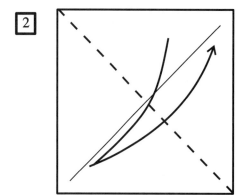

Valley-fold in half along the opposite diagonal and unfold.

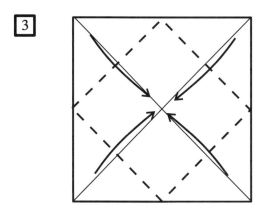

Blintz-fold the paper by valley-folding all the corners to the center.

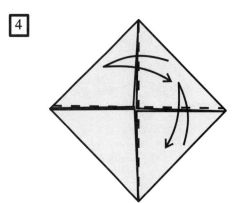

Valley-fold along the diagonals and unfold.

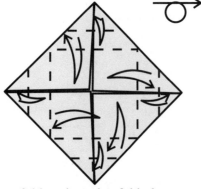

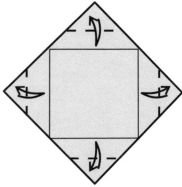

Blintz-fold again and unfold; then valley-fold all the corners to the creases. **Turn the model over.**

Valley-fold all the corners to the creases formed in step 5 and crease hard. Unfold only the corners. Turn the model so that it looks like step 7, which is an enlarged view.

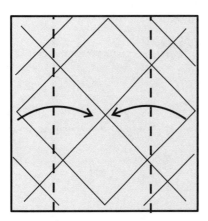

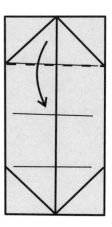

Enlarged view. The four corners of the original flat sheet are still in the center of the far side! Valley-fold the sides to the center.

Valley-fold the top edge to the center.

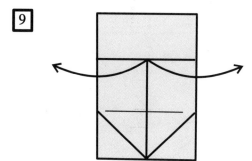

Grasp the two inner corners and pull them outward as far as they will go. Look ahead to step 10. Flatten the unit.

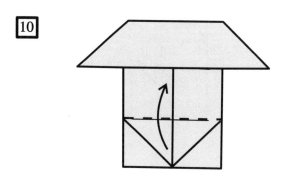

Repeat steps 8 and 9 on the bottom half.

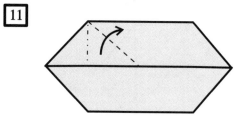

Lift the near top left corner of the base. Open it and squash-fold it down flat along the existing crease.

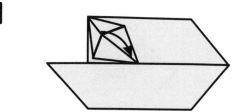

Step 12 shows the action of step 11 in progress. Flatten the new flap. Repeat step 11 on the three remaining corners.

13

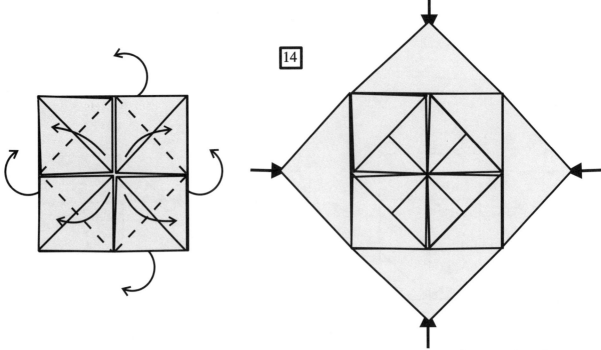

14

Enlarged view. Valley-fold the central corners of the near flaps to the outer corners of the model; then bring all four rear flaps outward from the back.

The Complex Base has eight large pockets. In most ornaments the four behind the side flaps will be used to connect the different parts of the ornaments.

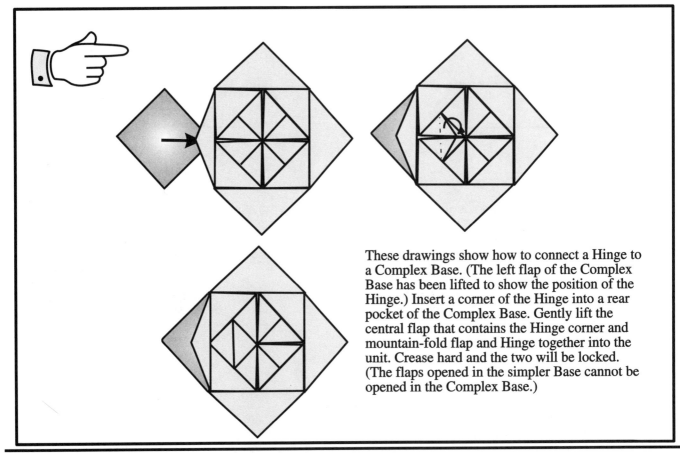

These drawings show how to connect a Hinge to a Complex Base. (The left flap of the Complex Base has been lifted to show the position of the Hinge.) Insert a corner of the Hinge into a rear pocket of the Complex Base. Gently lift the central flap that contains the Hinge corner and mountain-fold flap and Hinge together into the unit. Crease hard and the two will be locked. (The flaps opened in the simpler Base cannot be opened in the Complex Base.)

104 Complex Ornaments

Sturdy Cube

Fold six Complex Bases to make this interesting cube. Both front and back pockets of the base are used in this ornament. You may wish to add Inserts of foil or paper of a contrasting color. Remember to make these from the smaller squares of paper.

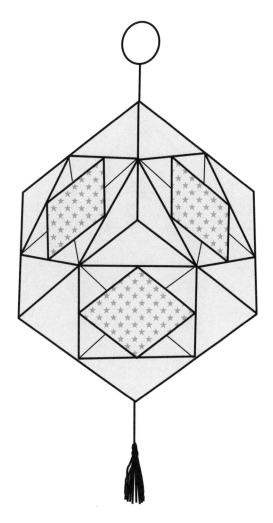

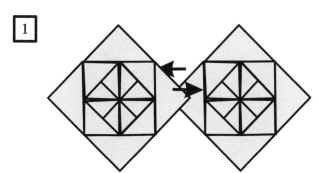

1

Insert the right flap of a Complex Base into the left front pocket of a second Complex Base. At the same time insert the left flap of the second unit into the back pocket of the first. Lock both flaps in the usual way.

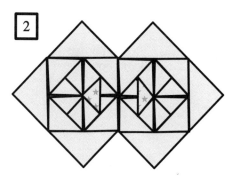

2

Repeat step 1 with two more Complex Bases.

3

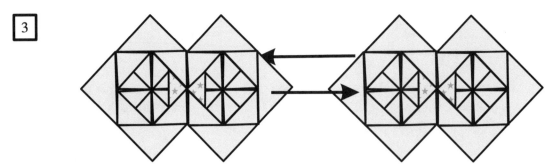

Fasten together the two assemblies made in steps 1 and 2 using the same method of locking.

4

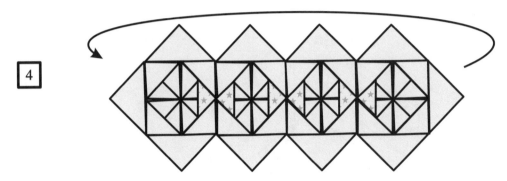

Swing the far right end backward to the left; join the right and left units in the way shown in step 1, completing an open box.

5

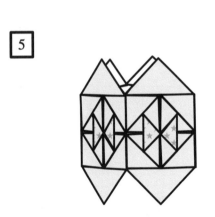

The open box needs to have a lid and bottom to complete the cube.

6

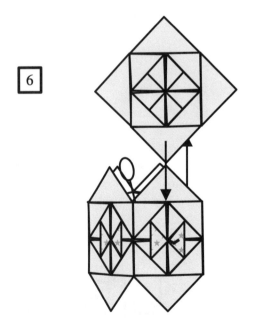

Begin adding a lid by inserting a flap from a fifth Complex Base into the upper front pocket of the open box while you insert the matching box flap into the lower back pocket of the fifth Complex Base. If you intend to hang the ornament, insert a looped string under a flap in the front before you lock both flaps.

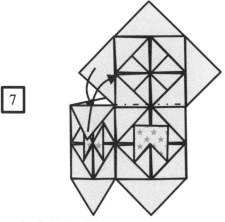

Mountain-fold the fifth base gently down onto the
open box and carefully insert and lock each side. Refer
to the suggestion box for help. Repeat steps 6 and 7 on
the bottom with another Complex Base. If you wish to
have a string tassel add it to the opposite corner from
the looped string and lock.

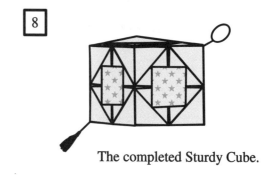

The completed Sturdy Cube.

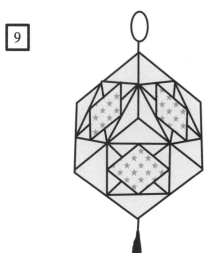

As you work your way around the open box, you will
have to curl the flaps in order to insert them into the
top or bottom Complex Base. The bottom pocket is the
problem because you cannot move any side flaps out
of the way. The top pocket will open to receive the
locking flap in the same way as it does in the Simple
Ornaments.

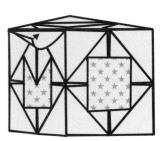

Lightstar Cube

This ornament requires sixteen squares of paper. Fold six Lightstar Bases (instructions follow). Then, using foil or paper of a contrasting color, fold six Joiners, two Hanging Joiners, and cut six Inserts. Fold the Lightstar Bases with the Inserts in place.

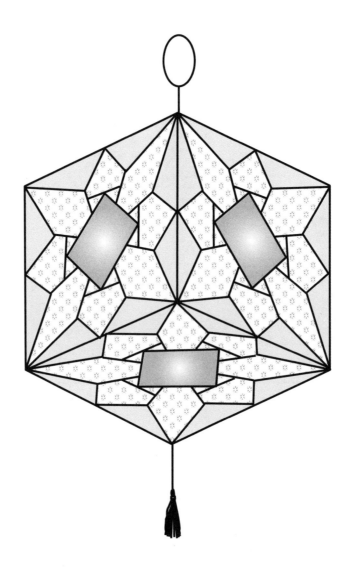

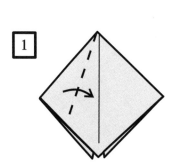

1 Begin a Hanging Joiner by folding through step 11 of the Clip on pages 11 and 12. Valley-fold the top left edge of this Joiner over to the centerline.

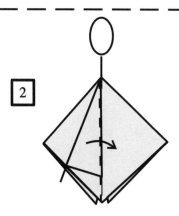

2 Insert a looped string under the nearest flap and place it directly into the crease at the left. Valley-fold the entire near left flap to the right over the centerline along with the string.

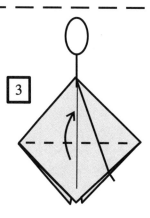

3 Valley-fold the near bottom corner to the top corner.

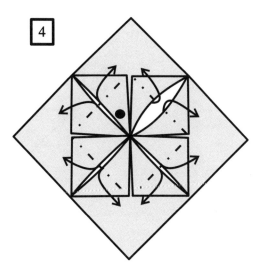

4 Begin with step 13 of the Complex Base (page 103). Bring all four rear flaps outward from the back. Open out the diagonal slit in each near flap; pull the edges as far apart as possible and flatten each flap outward. Watch the black dot.

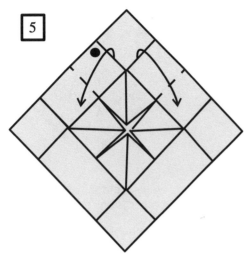

5

Valley-fold the two near top flaps
downward; the creases already exist.

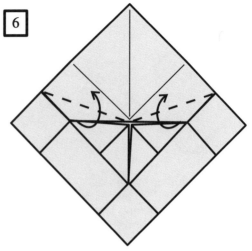

6

Lift only the near lower flaps of the upper
half of the unit and valley-fold them upward.

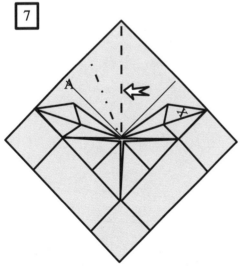

7

Swivel the vertical valley-fold counterclockwise so that it
lies directly behind crease A. Watch the spot marked X.
Flatten the unit.

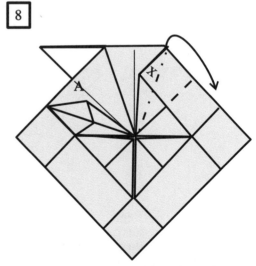

8

Return the unit to the position shown in step 7
by swiveling the upper right corner clockwise.
Watch the spot marked X.

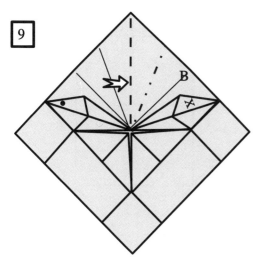

9

Swivel the vertical valley fold clockwise so that it lies directly behind crease B. Watch the black dot. Flatten the unit.

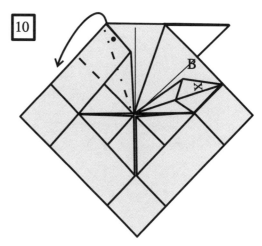

10

Return the unit to the position shown in step 9 by swiveling the upper left corner counterclockwise. Watch the black dot. Flatten the unit.

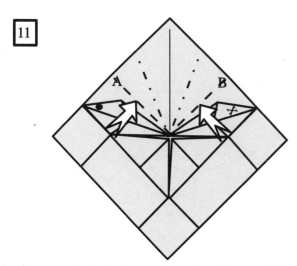

11

Push crease A clockwise as far as it will go and flatten. Push crease B counterclockwise as far as it will go and flatten. (The small flaps with a black dot and an X will move automatically into position behind the larger central flap.)

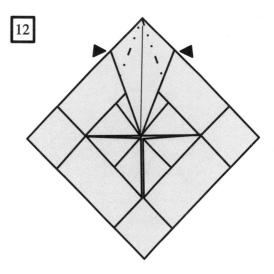

12

Reverse-fold the upper sides of the top near flap, forming a diamond shape.

13

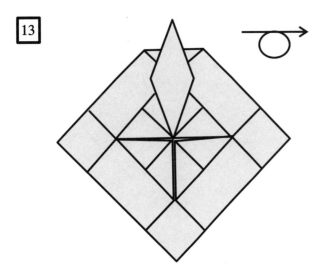

Turn the unit over.

14

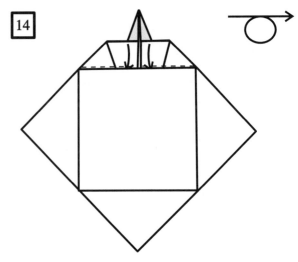

Valley fold the top flaps down into the near pocket. **Turn the unit over.**

15

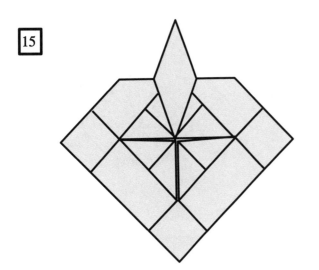

16

The Lightstar Base is ready for assembly.

Repeat steps 5–14 on each of the three remaining sides.

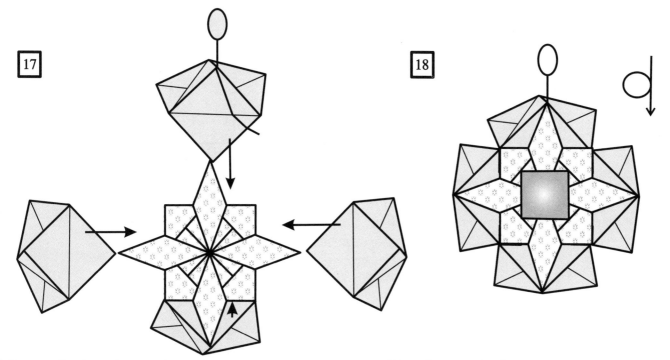

17

Insert a flap from the Hanging Joiner made in steps 1–3; add three more Joiners to one of the Lightstar Bases and lock.

18

Turn the completed assembly over onto a flat surface with the Lightstar Base on the bottom.

19

Add another Lightstar Base to one side of the assembly made in step 18. Mountain-fold to lock the Joiners to the base.

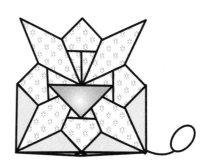

20

Add a Lightstar Base to each of the three remaining sides to form an open box.

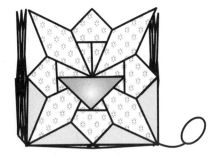

Place the completed assembly on a flat surface so that the top of the box is open.

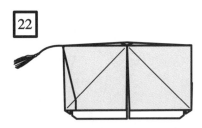

Complete another assembly by repeating steps 17–18. This assembly will form the top for the box. You may wish to include a tassel on one of the joiners opposite to the loop.

Join the completed parts from steps 21–22.

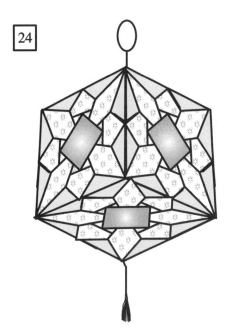

The Lightstar Cube is identical in structure to the Magic Cube found in the Simple Ornaments section. Although the only difference is the use of the Complex Base and the size of the paper, the two ornaments are quite different in appearance.

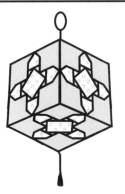

Magic Cube

Lightstar Cube

Lightstar Lantern

Fold three Lightstar Bases, one Flat Joiner (instructions below), three Hinges, and a Hanging Joiner (page 43). You may also wish to add Inserts to the Bases.

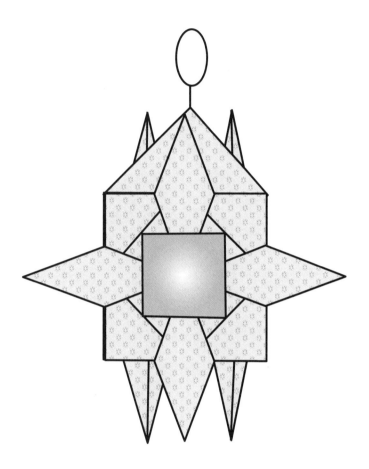

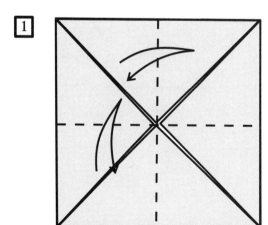

1

To make a Flat Joiner, begin with step 3 of the Clip (page 11). Valley-fold the square in half in both directions and unfold.

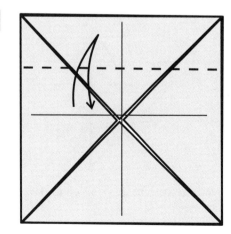

2

Valley-fold the top edge down to the centerline and unfold.

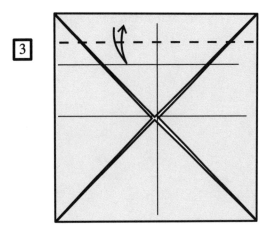

Valley-fold the top edge down to the crease made in step 2 and unfold.

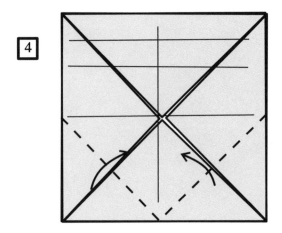

Valley-fold the bottom corners up to the centerpoint.

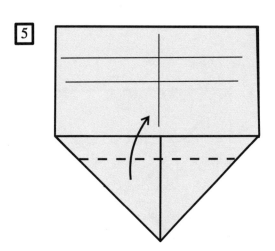

Valley-fold the bottom point up to the crease formed in step 2.

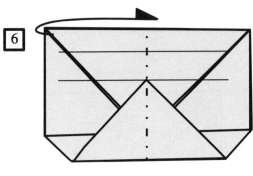

Mountain-fold in half.

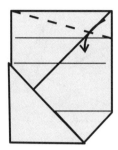 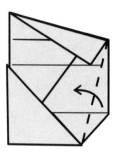

Valley-fold the top right corner from the left edge down to the point where the crease formed in step 3 meets the right edge. Repeat behind.

Valley-fold the right edge from the top right corner down to the bottom right corner. Repeat behind.

  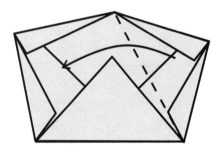

Swing the back flap leftward to its original position.

Valley-fold the right corner from the top center to the bottom right corner.

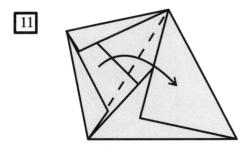

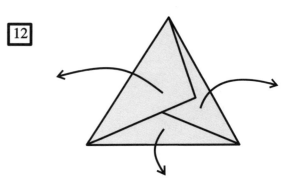

Repeat step 10 on the left side.

Open the three flaps.

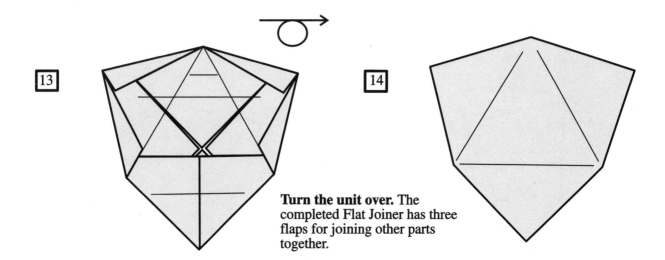

Turn the unit over. The completed Flat Joiner has three flaps for joining other parts together.

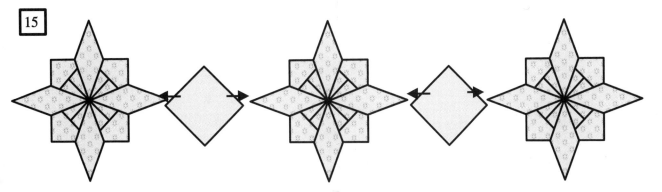

Join three Lightstar Bases with two Hinges and lock.

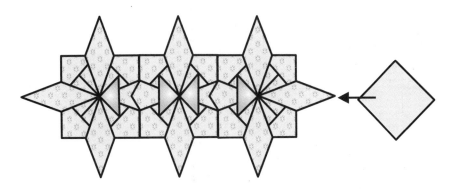

16

Add another Hinge and lock.

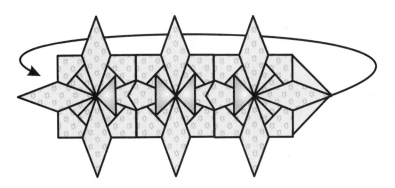

Swing the far right end of the assembly backward to the left; insert the right Lightstar Base into the left and lock.

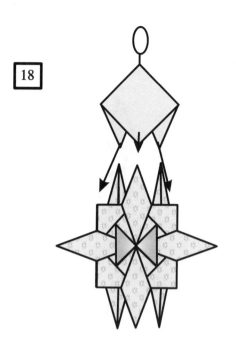

18

Insert the three flaps of the Hanging Joiner into the lantern and lock.

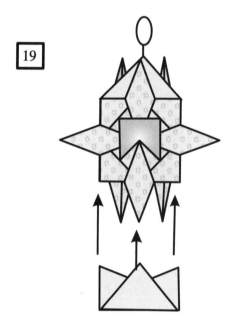

19

The bottom of this lantern will be flat. Lock a Flat Joiner to the lantern assembly.

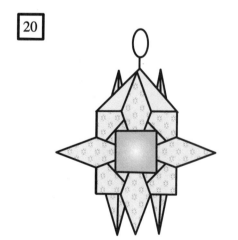

20

The Lightstar Lantern is much different in appearance from the earlier lanterns.

Complex Ball

Fold six Complex Bases. Then, using foil or paper of a contrasting color, fold eight Flat Joiners (page 115) to make this ball ornament. You may wish to add Inserts to the Complex Bases. Fold the Complex Bases with the Inserts in place.

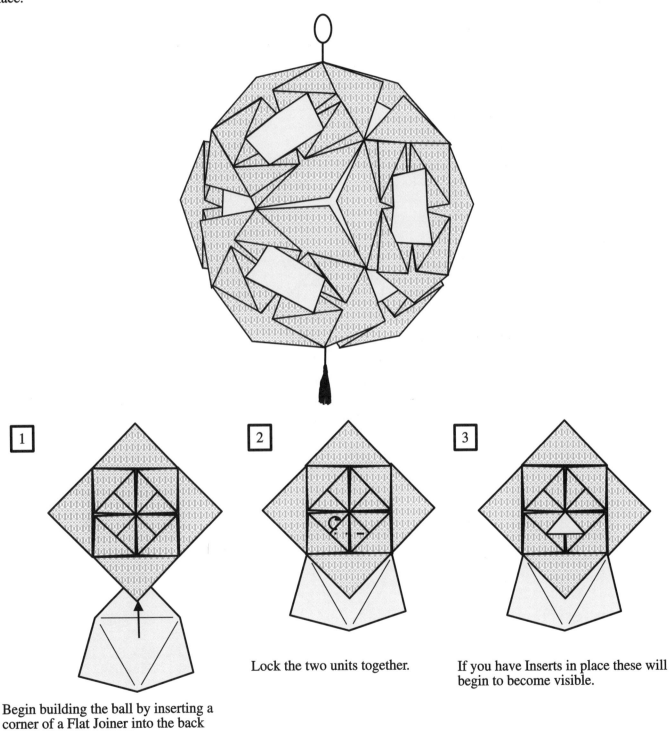

1 Begin building the ball by inserting a corner of a Flat Joiner into the back pocket of a Complex Base.

2 Lock the two units together.

3 If you have Inserts in place these will begin to become visible.

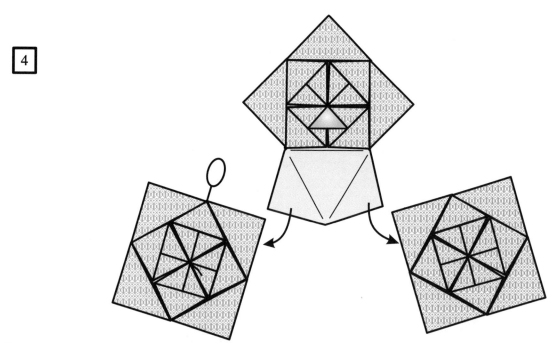

Join two more Complex Bases to the Flat Joiner. You will need to pick up the models to assemble them. Center each Flat Joiner in its pocket and then lock. If you are going to add a looped string, add it before you lock.

5

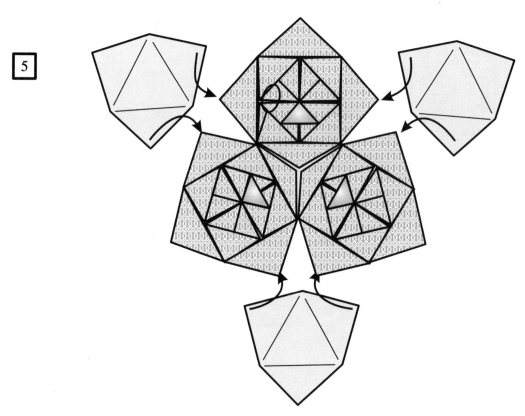

Add three more Flat Joiners to the assembly. You will need to hold the assembly as you add each Joiner. Each Joiner will have two flaps to insert and lock. When you have joined the units they will form a hollow bowl.

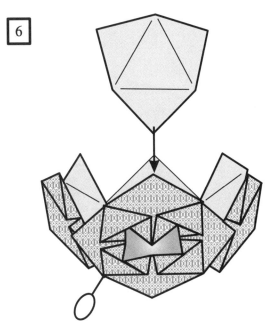

6

Add a Flat Joiner to one of the bases on the bowl-shaped assembly.

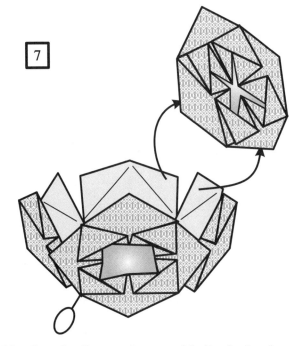

7

Add a Complex Base to the assembly. Look ahead to step 8.

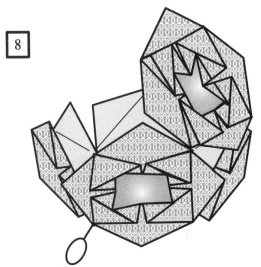

8

Work your way around the bowl, adding a Flat Joiner and then a Base until you have added three of each.

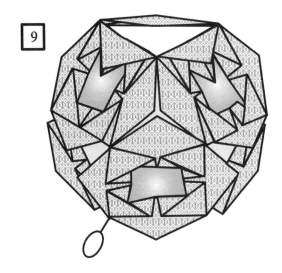

9

The resulting model will have a total of six Bases, and seven Flat Joiners. If you plan to add potpourri to the ball, you should do it now. If you plan to hang your ball, you will need to add the string to the assembly before the final step.

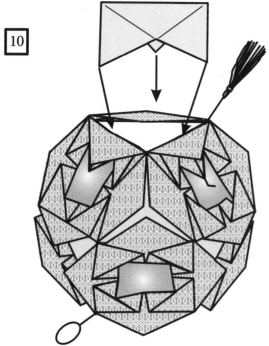

10

11

Add each flap of the remaining Flat Joiner to the assembly. The Joiner flaps must remain on the outside of the assembly as each is locked into a Complex Base. If you are going to add a string tassel, do it before the final locking.

All of the Complex Balls are assembled in the same manner. The Complex Bases can be folded in different patterns, but the assembly of the ball (Cuboctahedron) remains the same.

Looped strings for hanging the ornaments have to be added during the assembly. They are either added to a Hanging Joiner or inserted under one of the side flaps on the Complex Bases. The string must be long enough to be folded under when the flap is locked into position. String tassels can be added to the opposite side of the ornament in the same manner. Complex Bases that have been folded into different patterns require a different method of attaching a string. The end of the string must be tied to a scrap of paper and placed between the joiners and base. When the Joiners are locked into the Complex Base, both string and paper are trapped between the different parts of the ball. This procedure is explained in the next ornament.

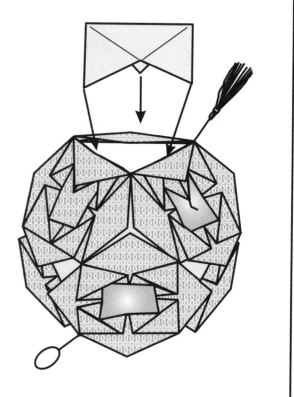

Starbright Ball

Fold six Complex Bases of the Starbright type (instructions follow). Then, using foil or paper of a contrasting color, fold eight Flat Joiners (page 112). You may wish to add Inserts to the Starbright Bases. Fold the Starbright Bases with the Inserts in place.

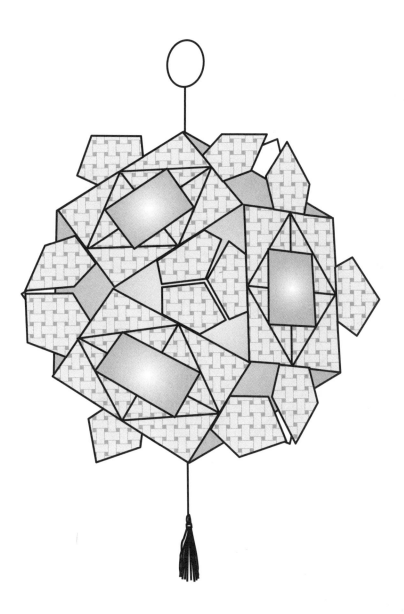

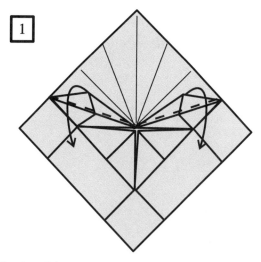

1

Begin with step 11 of the Lightstar Base
(page 109). Swing the near triangular
flaps down as shown.

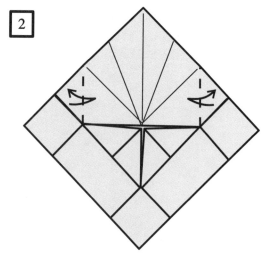

2

Valley-fold the two near corners of the near
flap along existing creases as shown; unfold.

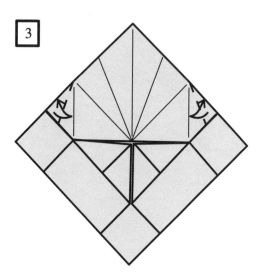

3

Valley-fold the outer edges of the two corners to
the crease lines formed in step 2; **unfold**.

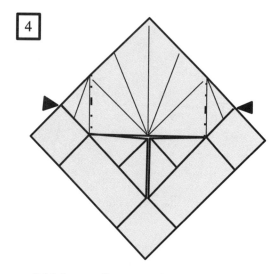

4

Reverse-fold the small corners into the near top flap.

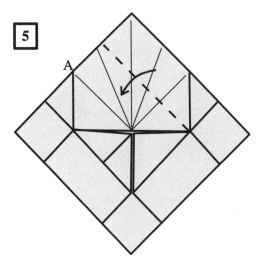

5

Valley-fold and the top corner to point A and flatten.

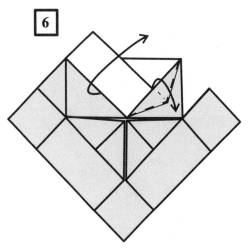

6

Pull downward and to the right the raw edge of the small triangle as you return the larger flap to its former position. All of the creases already exist.

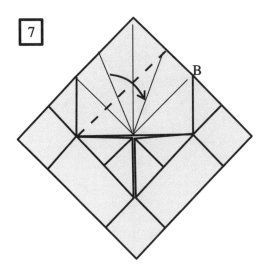

7

Valley-fold the top corner to point B and flatten.

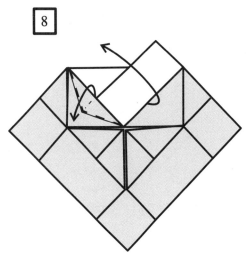

8

Repeat the actions of step 6 on the left half of the unit.

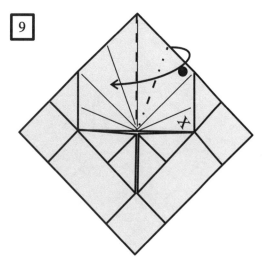

9

Pull the existing mountain crease counterclockwise as far as it will go. Watch the black dot and the X.

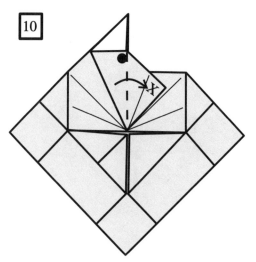

10

Swing the top near flap rightward along the centerline.

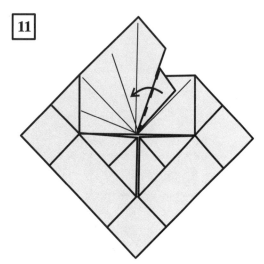

11

Valley-fold the small flap leftward. Look ahead to step 12.

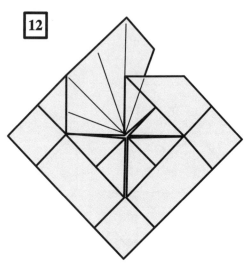

12

The actions of steps 9–11 create one side of an extended flap, formed now on the inside of the base.

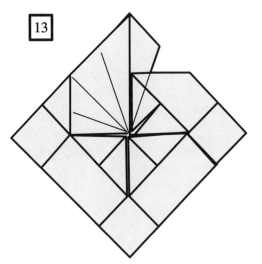

13

Repeat steps 9–12 on the left side
of the top near flap.

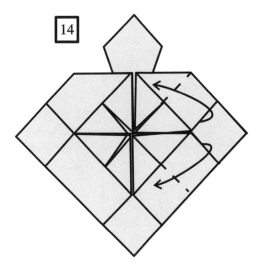

14

Valley-fold the near right flaps as shown. Then repeat steps
5 through 13 on the right. Do the same with the bottom and
left corner of the Complex Base.

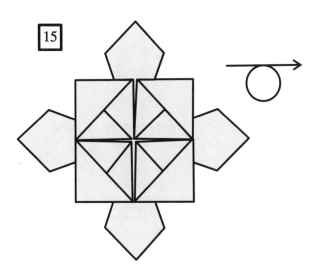

15

Turn the model over.

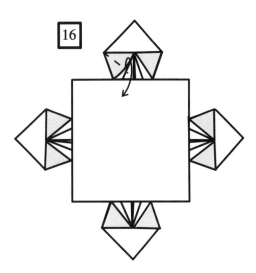

16

Open out the top left near flap and flatten downward onto
the back of the Base. Look ahead to step 17.

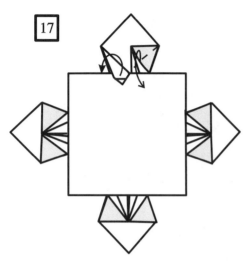

Tuck the bottom of the flap down into the pocket and repeat steps 16–17 on the seven remaining near flaps.

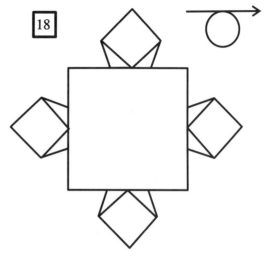

Turn the model over.

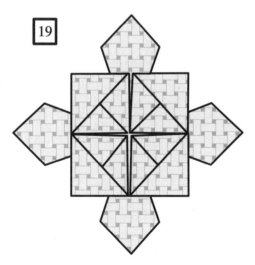

The Starbright Base is ready for assembly.

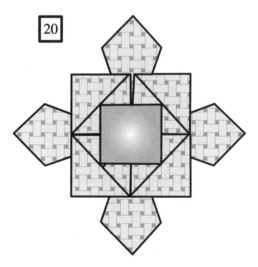

Here is the Starbright Base as it appears with an Insert.

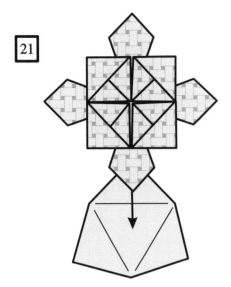

Begin building the ball by inserting a corner of a Flat Joiner into the back pocket of a Starbright Base.

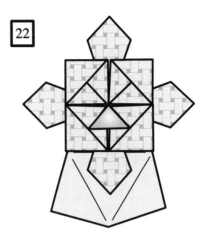

With the corner of the Flat Joiner in the pocket, lock the two units together.

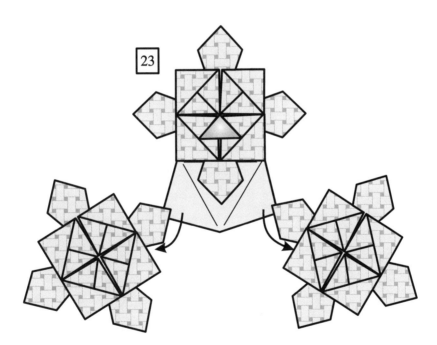

Lock two more Starbright Bases onto the Flat Joiner. You will need to pick up the models as you assemble them. Adjust each Flat Joiner flap to center it in the pocket; then mountain-fold to lock the units together.

Add three more Flat Joiners to the assembly. Each Flat Joiner will have two flaps to insert and lock onto the Starbright Bases. You will need to hold the assembled units as you add each Flat Joiner. When you have joined the models together they will form a hollow bowl. When the Complex Base is folded into different patterns, you will need to tie a small scrap of paper to the end of the looped string and place it between the Joiner and Complex Base as you assemble the various balls. Be sure that the end with the scrap of paper goes to the inside of the ornament.

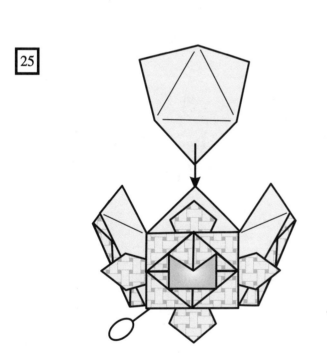

Add a Flat Joiner to one of the Starbright Bases of the bowl-shaped assembly.

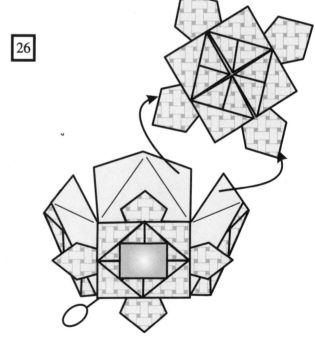

Add a Starbright Base to the assembly. Look ahead to step 27.

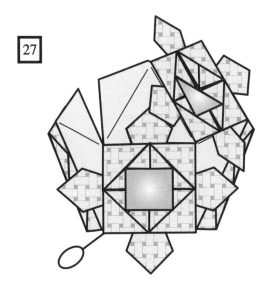

27

Work your way around the bowl, adding a
Flat Joiner and then a Starbright Base until
you have added three of each.

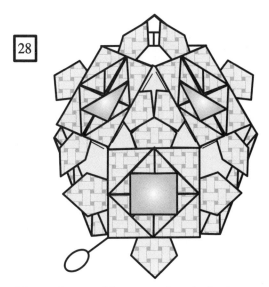

28

If you plan to add potpourri to the ball, you
should do it now.

29

Add each flap of the remaining Flat Joiner to the
assembly. The Flat Joiner flaps must remain on the
outside of the assembly as each is locked into the
Starbright Base. If you wish to add a string tassel to
the ornament, do it before the final locking.

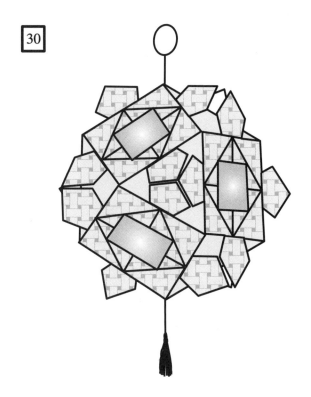

30

All of the Complex Balls are assembled in the same
manner. The Complex Bases can be folded in different
patterns, but the assembly of the ball (Cuboctahedron)
remains the same.

Starlight Oddball

Fold six Starlight Bases (instructions below). Then, using foil or paper of a contrasting color, fold three Double Flat Joiners (instructions below), two Hanging Joiners and three Hinges to make this ball. You may wish to add Inserts of a contrasting color.

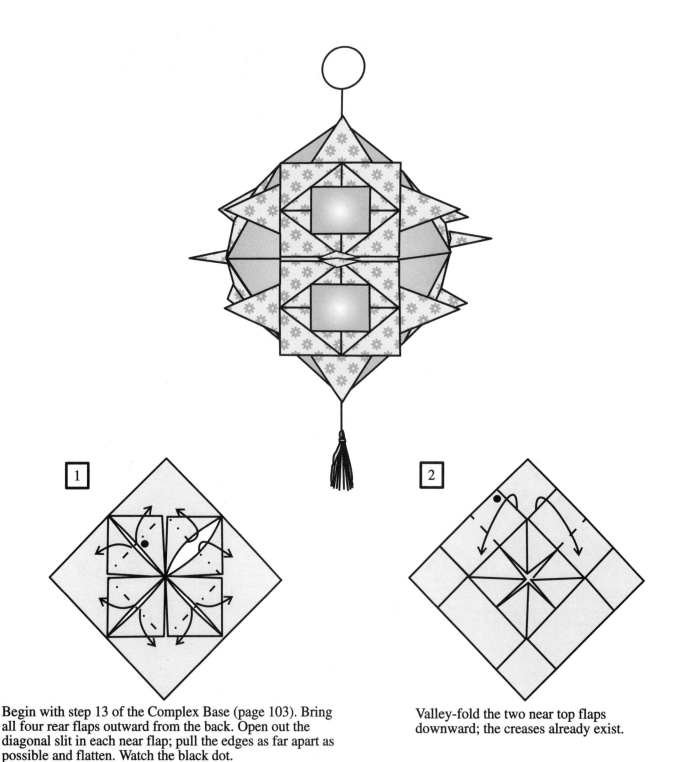

1

Begin with step 13 of the Complex Base (page 103). Bring all four rear flaps outward from the back. Open out the diagonal slit in each near flap; pull the edges as far apart as possible and flatten. Watch the black dot.

2

Valley-fold the two near top flaps downward; the creases already exist.

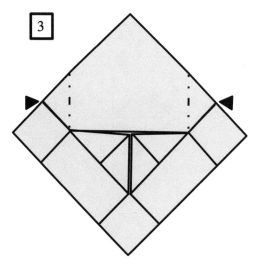

3

Reverse-fold the two near corners inward; the creases already exist.

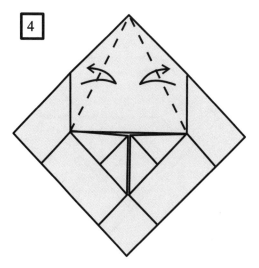

4

Valley-fold the near top flap so that the crease runs from the top point down to the lower corners as shown. Unfold.

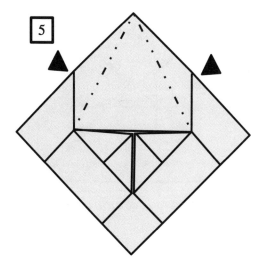

5

Reverse-fold inward the sides of the near flap; the creases already exist.

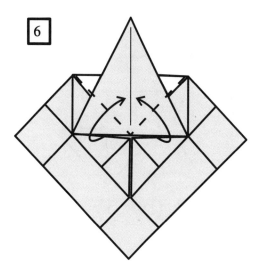

6

Valley-fold the lower corners of the near flap upward to the vertical centerline.

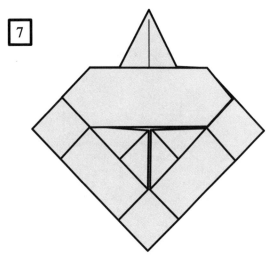

7

Repeat steps 2–6 on the three remaining sides.

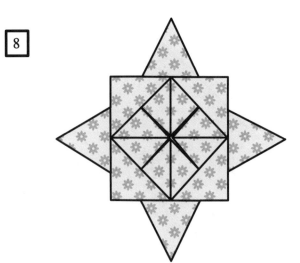

8

The Starlight Base is ready for assembly.

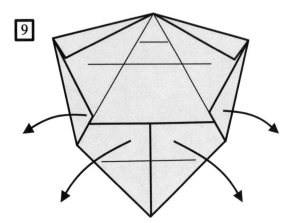

9

Make a Flat Tandem Joiner by beginning with a Flat Joiner (page 112). Unfold the side and bottom flaps.

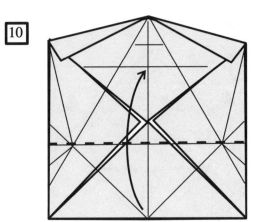

10

Valley-fold the bottom edge upward along the existing crease.

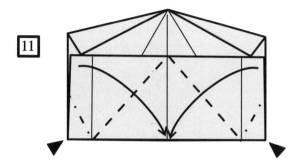

11

Valley-fold so that the two halves of the horizontal raw edge lie along the centerline. The small mountain creases will form themselves as the sides are flattened. Look ahead to step 12.

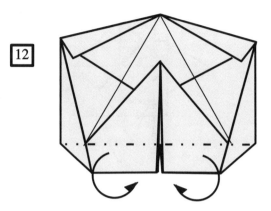

12

Mountain-fold the bottom edges up into the pocket behind them. This will complete the Flat Tandem Joiner.

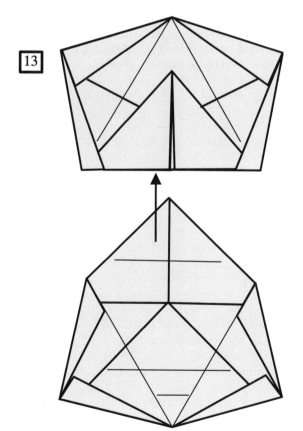

13

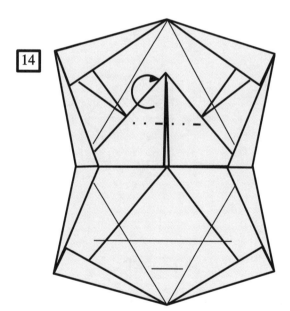

14

To make a Double Flat Joiner, insert the double-layer flap from a Flat Joiner into the pocket of the Flat Tandem Joiner and lock the two together by mountain-folding the resulting triangular flap as shown. The drawings show the back of the assembly.

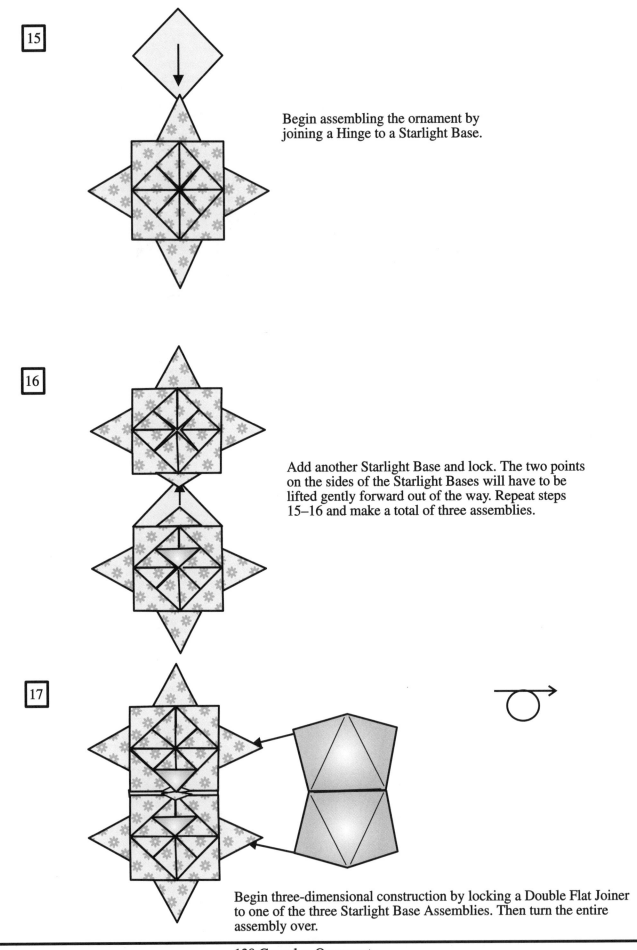

15

Begin assembling the ornament by
joining a Hinge to a Starlight Base.

16

Add another Starlight Base and lock. The two points
on the sides of the Starlight Bases will have to be
lifted gently forward out of the way. Repeat steps
15–16 and make a total of three assemblies.

17

Begin three-dimensional construction by locking a Double Flat Joiner
to one of the three Starlight Base Assemblies. Then turn the entire
assembly over.

18

Add a Hanging Joiner (page 43) to the
top and bottom of the assembly. If you
want to add a looped string and string
tassel you must do it before adding the
Hanging Joiners.

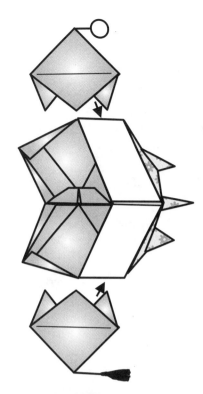

19

Add a second Base assembly
by locking in place the two
Hanging Joiners and the
sides of the Double Flat
Joiners.

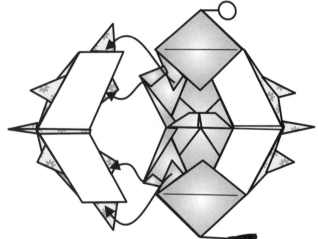

20

Add a Double Flat Joiner to the
ornament and lock.

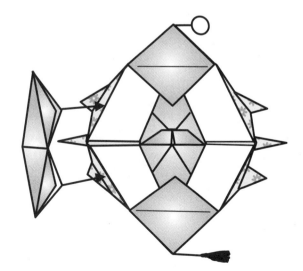

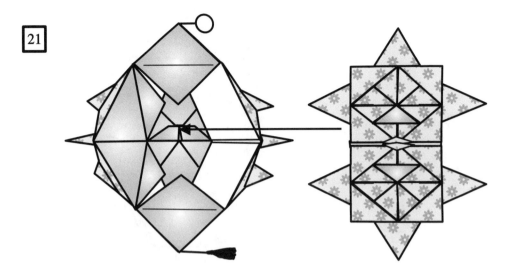

21

Add the last Starlight Base assembly to the ornament and lock.

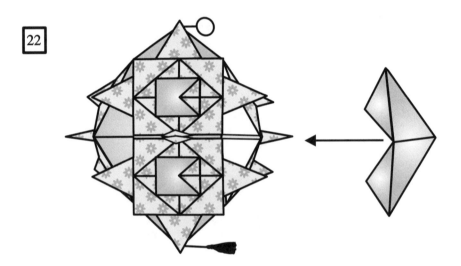

22

Finish the ornament by adding a Double Flat Joiner.

23

Complex Starlight Cube

Fold six Starlight Bases, and eight Three-Sided Complex Bases (instructions below) before assembling this model. You may wish to add Inserts to the Bases to enhance the appearance of the ornament.

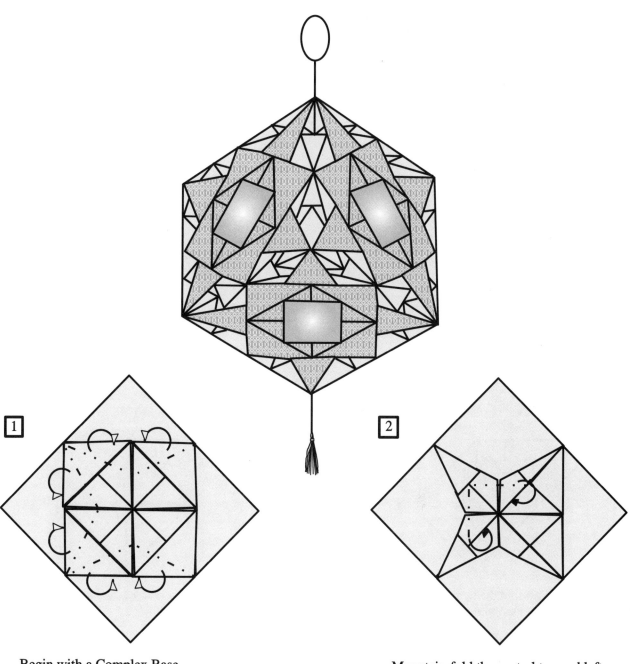

1. Begin with a Complex Base. Mountain-fold the outer edges of the near flaps as shown. These folds are the same as those of the Four-Pointed Star pattern (page 37).

2. Mountain-fold the central top and left flaps inside the model. This is the same procedure as locking a flap to a Base.

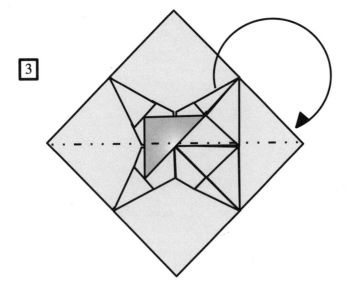

3

Mountain-fold the model downward in
half.

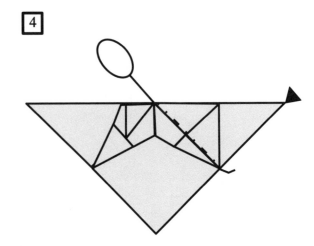

4

Reverse-fold the upper right corner
downward. If you are going to add a looped
string or tassel to the ornament, insert it
under the near right flap.

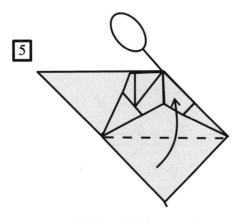

5

Valley-fold the near bottom
flap to the top.

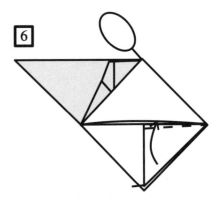

6

Valley-fold the inner flap up into the
pocket behind the near flap.

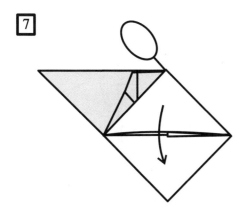

7

Swing the near top flap back down.

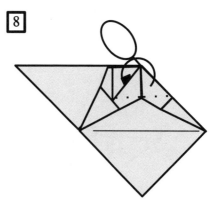

8

Mountain-fold the near flaps inside the model. This is the same procedure as locking a flap to a Base.

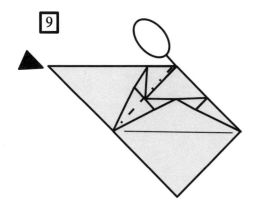

9

Reverse-fold the top left flap downward.

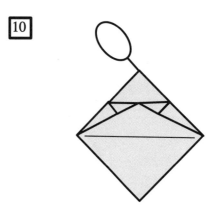

10

Open up the model from the bottom into a Complex Three-sided Base.

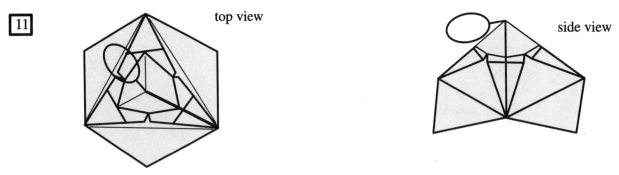

top view   side view

The finished Complex Three-Sided Base can be used as a Joiner, or as a separate Base to build more complex ornaments.

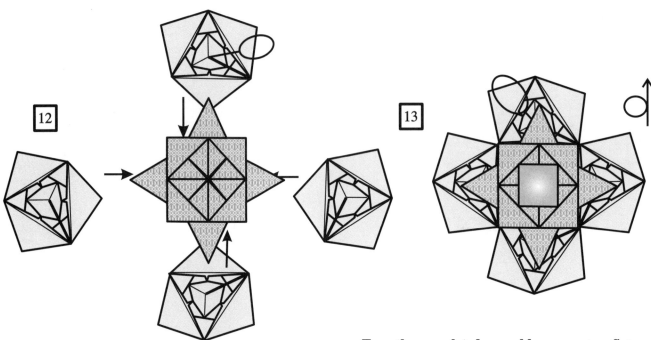

Join four Three-Sided Complex Bases onto a Starlight Base (page 128). Then mountain-fold the center flaps of the Starlight Base inward, locking the assembly together.

Turn the completed assembly over onto a flat surface with the Starlight Base on the bottom.

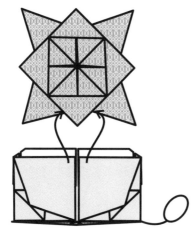

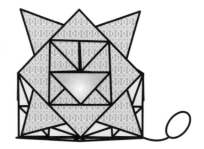

Add a Starlight Base to one side of the assembly. Insert the flaps of the Three-Sided Complex Bases into the Starlight Base and lock.

Add a Starlight Base to each of the three remaining sides to form an open box.

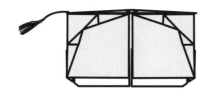

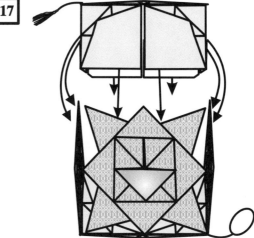

Complete another assembly by repeating steps 12 and 13. This assembly will form the top of the box. You may wish to include a tassel on one of the joiners opposite the loop used to hang the Cube.

Join the completed parts from steps 15 and 16.

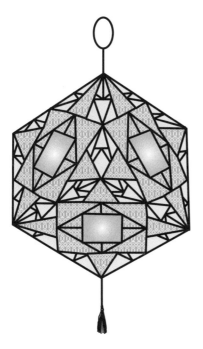

Four-Sided Brightstar Carousel

Fold four Brightstar Ornament Bases (instructions below). Then, using foil or paper of a contrasting color, fold two Four-Sided Flat Joiners (instructions below), and four Hinges. You may wish to add Inserts to the Bases to enhance the appearance of the ornament.

1

Begin with step 19 of the Starbright Base (page 124). Tuck the near top inner flaps into the pockets behind them. Look ahead to step 2.

2

Repeat step 1 on the remaining three sides.

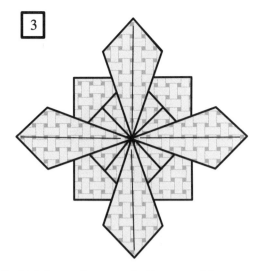

3

The Brightstar Base ready for assembly.

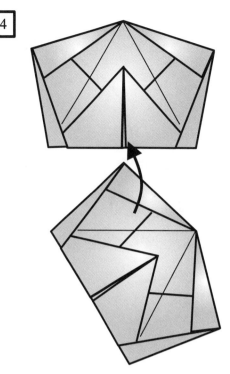

4

Begin making a Four-Sided Flat Joiner by inserting one Flat Tandem Joiner into another. Lock.

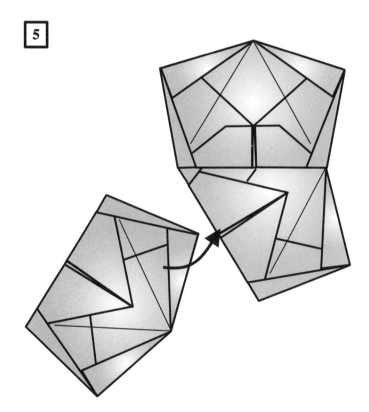

5

Lock to the assembly a third Flat Tandem Joiner.

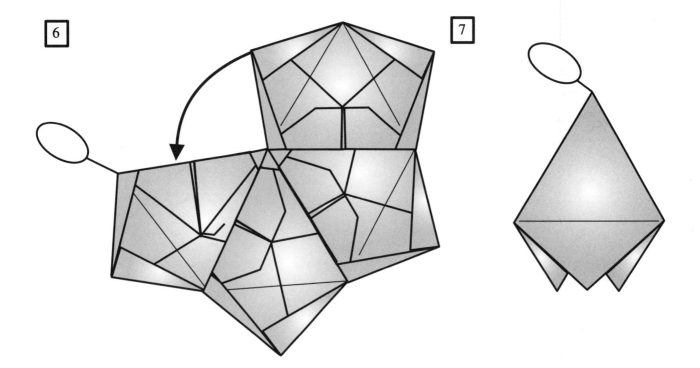

6 Lock to the assembly a fourth Flat Tandem Joiner. Hold the assembly in your hands and shape it into a pyramid. If you are going to add a looped string add it now. Insert and lock the remaining flap, to complete the Four-Sided Flat Joiner.

7 Make a second Four-Sided Flat Joiner. If you are going to add a string tassel to the ornament, don't forget to add it to the last step. The Four-Sided Flat Joiner can join four Complex Bases.

8 Begin assembling the ornament by locking together four Brightstar Bases and four Hinges. The points on the stars will have to be lifted gently forward as each is added to the chain of bases.

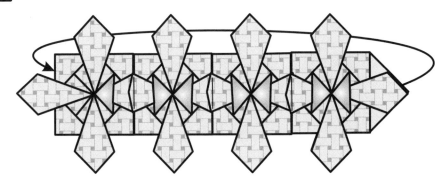

Swing the far right end of the assembly backward to the left; insert and lock the right base into the left, forming an open box.

The bases have been folded into a ring and only the top and bottom of the carousel remain to be assembled.

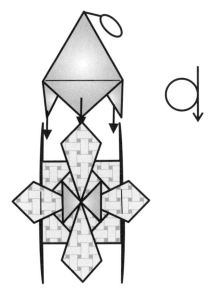

11

Add a Four-Sided Flat Joiner to the ring. This is one of the most difficult ornaments to assemble because the flaps of the Four-Sided Flat Joiner must be inserted into the back pockets of each base and locked. If patience is a virtue you are about to test your own. Good Luck! **Turn the model over.**

12

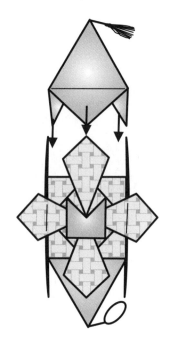

Add the final Four-Sided Flat Joiner to complete this difficult but satisfying ornament.

Designing Ornaments

Tristar Lantern

All of the units in this book are interchangeable. You may choose any Clip, Joiner, or type of Base to construct your ornament. Here is an example using the Tristar Clip (page 77) with the Hanging Joiners to make a lantern. Follow the instructions for making the Lantern (page 85), but substitute the Tristar Clip for the original simple Clip. This ornament requires eight squares the same size. Fold three Bases (page 9); then, using foil or paper of a contrasting color, fold three Tristar Clips and two Hanging Joiners.

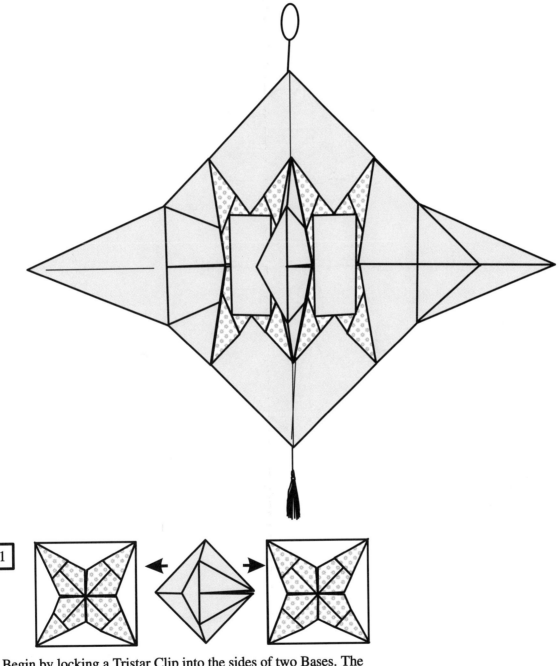

Begin by locking a Tristar Clip into the sides of two Bases. The illustration shows a Base folded into a Four-Pointed Star Pattern (page 37), but you may fold it into any pattern you wish.

2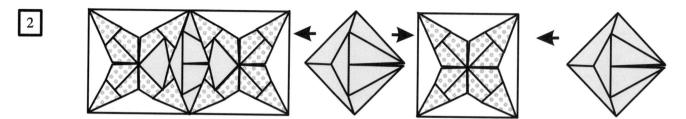

Join the assembly made in step 1 to another Tristar Clip and another Base. Insert one flap of a third Tristar Clip into the last Base and lock.

3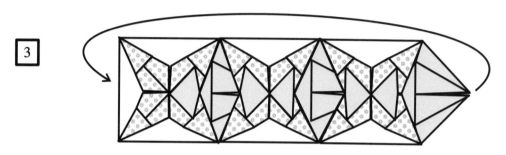

Swing the far right end of the assembly backward to the left to form an open three-sided ring; lock the right flaps into the left base.

4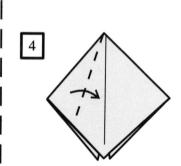

Form a Hanging Joiner by folding through step 12 of the Clip on page 12.

5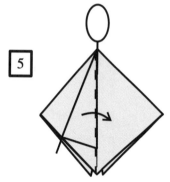

Insert a looped string under the nearest flap and place it directly into the crease at the left. Valley-fold the entire near left flap to the right over the centerline along with the string.

6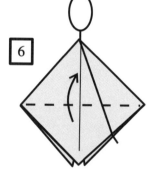

Valley-fold the bottom corner of the near flap all the way up to the top corner. Repeat on the two remaining flaps. Open the Hanging Joiner when you are ready to lock it onto the ornament. Do this by bringing the three flaps downward again and opening out the rear flaps from below.

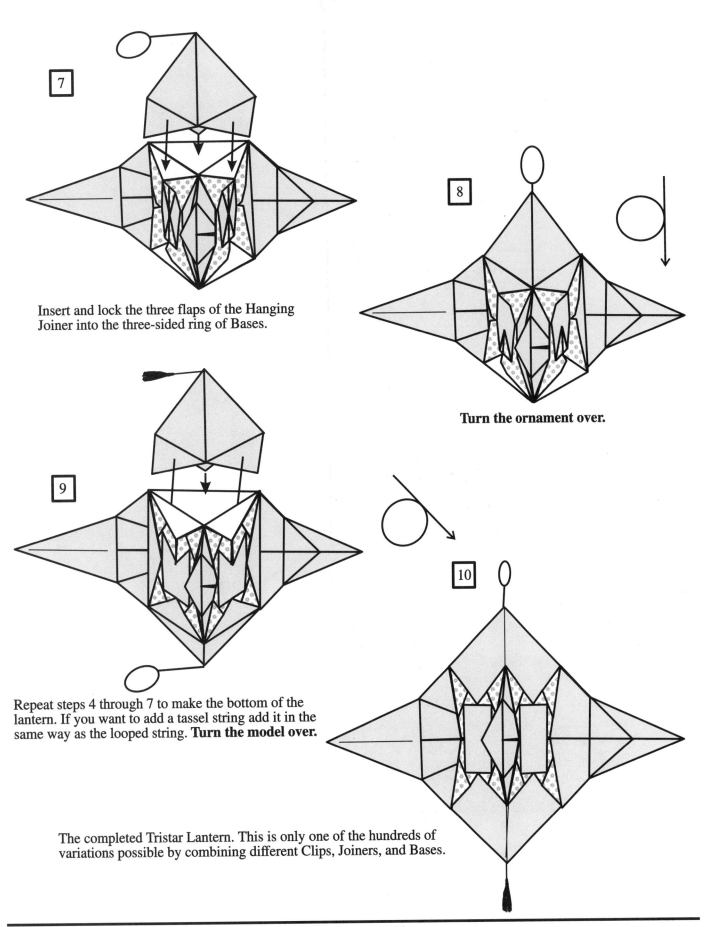

7

Insert and lock the three flaps of the Hanging Joiner into the three-sided ring of Bases.

8

Turn the ornament over.

9

Repeat steps 4 through 7 to make the bottom of the lantern. If you want to add a tassel string add it in the same way as the looped string. **Turn the model over.**

10

The completed Tristar Lantern. This is only one of the hundreds of variations possible by combining different Clips, Joiners, and Bases.

Tristar Cube

Here is another variation using the Tristar Clip. Substitute the Tristar Clip for the simple Clip and make the Cube (page 40). This ornament requires twenty squares the same size. Fold six Bases; then, using foil or paper of a contrasting color, fold twelve Tristar Clips, and cut six Inserts for the Bases. Fold the Bases with the Inserts in place.

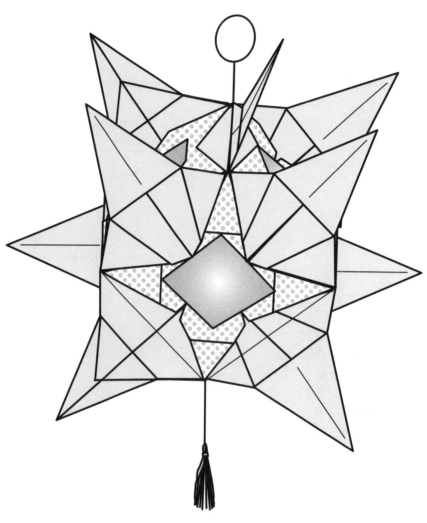

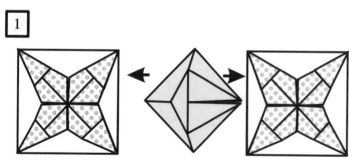

Insert the flaps of a Tristar Clip into the sides of two Bases and lock.

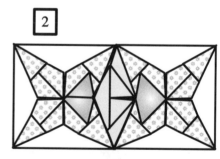

Repeat step 1 with a Tristar Clip and two more Bases. Continue with the instructions from step 3 on page 41, substituting the Tristar Clip for the Clip.

Six-Sided Carousel

You can create new and different ornaments. This Six-Sided Carousel is constructed the same way as the Five-sided Carousel (page 93) but has an added Tandem Joiner and another Base. This ornament requires twenty-two squares the same size. Fold six Bases; then, using foil or paper of a contrasting color, fold six Hinges and twelve Tandem Joiners, and cut six Inserts for the Bases. Fold the Bases with the Inserts in place.

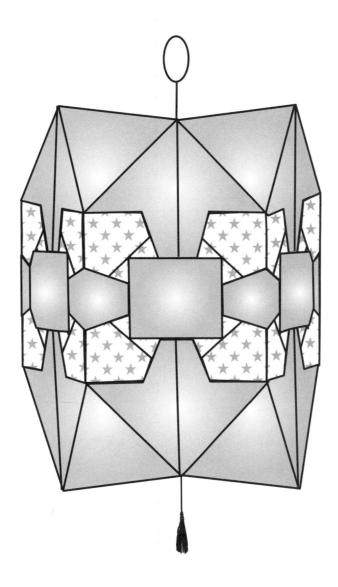

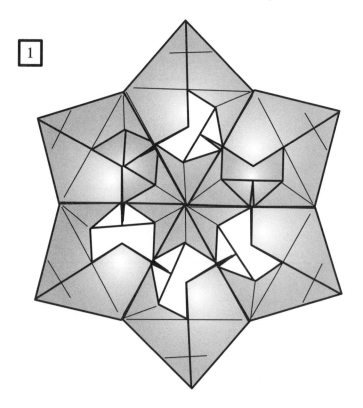

1

Proceed through step 2 of the Five-Sided Carousel. Add a sixth Tandem Joiner onto the Assembly.

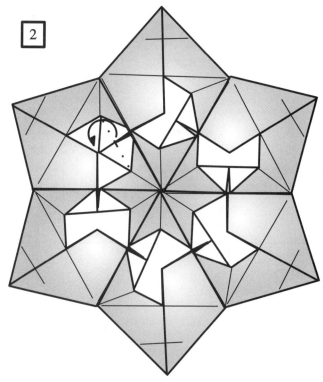

2

Pick up the assembly and hold it in your hands. Form the assembly into a concave bowl shape, and lock the sixth Joiner to the first one. If you intend to hang your ornament, insert a looped string before locking the final flap.

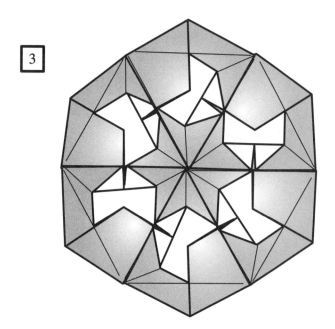

3

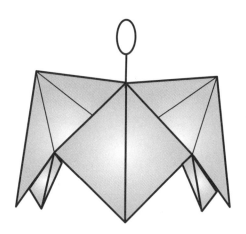

Step 3 shows the interior of the assembly and a side view. Make a second Tandem Joiner assembly. If you want to have a tassel, add it before locking down the last flap.

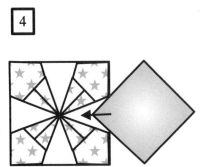

Insert a Hinge into a Base and lock.

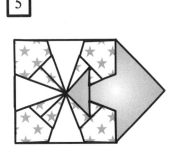

Make a chain as for the Five-Sided Carousel and add the assembly made in step 4, making a Six-Sided Carousel chain.

6

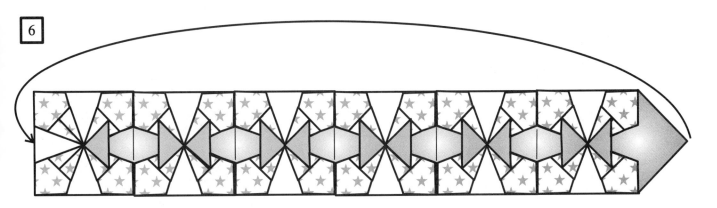

Swing the right end backward to the left; insert and lock the right Hinge into the left Base.

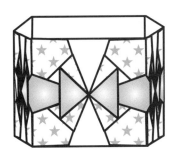

The six-sided ring.

8

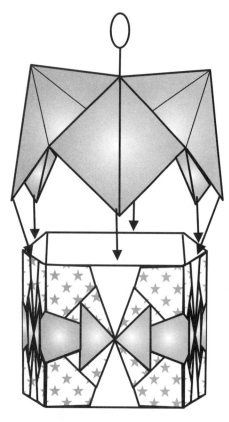

Insert and lock the six flaps of the Tandem Joiner assembly into the pockets of the six-sided ring.

9

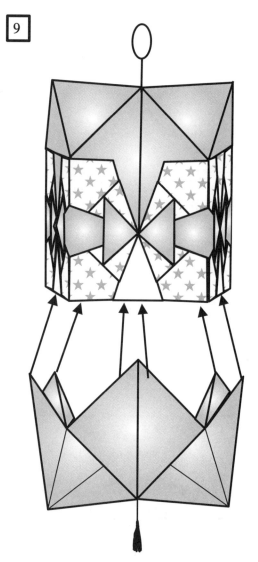

Insert the second Tandem Joiner assembly into the six-sided ring and lock it to complete the Six-Sided Carousel.

10

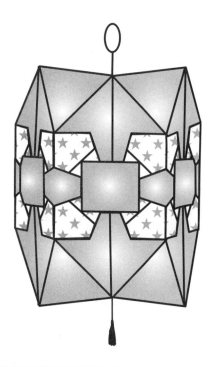

Six-Sided Brightstar Carousel

Try making a Six-Sided Brightstar Carousel [...] ;ed for the Four-Sided Brightstar Carousel (page 138). The Flat Joiners give t[...] te different from that of the Six-Sided Carousel. Fold six Brightstar Base[...] mblies (shown below), and six Hinges. You may wish to add Inserts to the E[...]

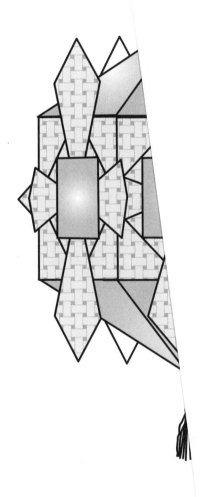

Follow the instructions for making the Four-Sided Brightstar C[...] ; a Four-Sided Flat Joiner use a Six-Sided Flat Joiner following the same procedu[...] :arousel. Although there are more Joiners, they assemble in the same way. Remen[...] tassel to complete the model.

Double Four-Sided Brightstar Carousel

Jackstone

Made from two Four-Sided Brightstar Carousels

Made from six Five-Sided Sturdy Cubes

Afterword

In this book we have been concerned with modular construction, or unit origami. These Kusudama are assemblies of units, and the units are elements of a system of folding. The balls presented here are only a few of the possibilities: the bases may be linked and locked together in countless ways waiting to be discovered. This system in turn is only one system, and modular construction is only one type of origami.

As Martin Gardner wrote some forty years ago, "After centuries of folding in the Orient, surely (one is tempted to think) the supply of such models must long ago have been exhausted. Far from it! . . . Such is not the case." Since then thousands of wonderful origami models have been created all over the world, and each one seems to suggest further creative paths. Origami is now everywhere in a quiet way. Any public library has a substantial collection of origami books. There are origami newsletters, origami clubs, and origami conventions – each of these, incidentally, the source of many lasting friendships. And the mighty resources of the Internet are readily available to paperfolders young and old.

This is a book without an ending. I hope that *Origami Ornaments* will serve as a gateway to the endlessly fascinating world of origami.

Internet Resources

!!!CAUTION!!!
Diagrams downloaded from an unknown source on the Internet may contain a virus.

My Favorite
http://library.thinkquest.org/27152/index.htm
Yurii and Katrin Shumakov's web site. Travel to Oriland. The world of Oriland has seven fantastic cities with huge collections of origami plus 70 diagrammed models. Seeing, reading and doing! Educational and fun.

Web Sites
http://www.origami.vancouver.bc.ca
The art of paper folding. Comprehensive collection of origami materials, instructions, and resources. Links to many other web pages.

Sources
http://www.concentric.net/~mikeinnj/orisrc.shtm
Janet Hamilton's List of Origami Sources

Societies
Britain
http://www.britishorigami.org.uk/
Italy
http://www.essenet.it/cdo/
Denmark
http://www.thok.dk/
USA
http://www.origami-usa.org/
Sweden
http://hem.passagen.se/dion
Japan (in Japanese)
http://origami.gr.jp/
France (in French)
http://www.multimania.com/osel/origami.htm

Paper and Book Supplies
http://www.fascinating-folds.com
World's largest supplier for origami and the paper arts
http://www.kimscrane.com
Supplier of origami books and papers from around the world
http://interlog.com/~washi/81%
Japanese Paper Place sells a selection of the fine Japanese papers and other products

Web Ring
http://nav.webring.org/hub?ring=origami;list
Joins pages about origami around the world

Interest Group
The Netherlands
http://www.rug.nl/rugcis/rc/ftp/origami/
Origami general interest group

Visit Me, Lew Rozelle, at
http://members.aol.com/judithrcns/index.htm

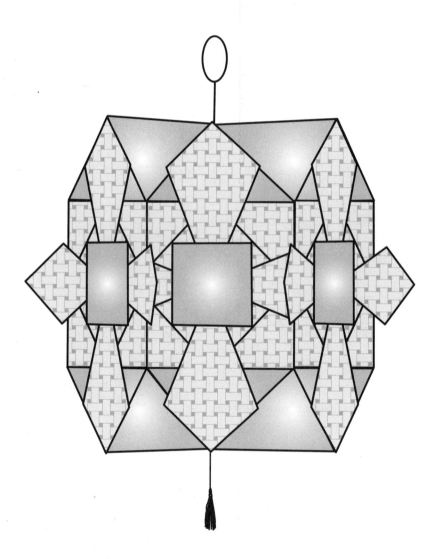